Praise for
Walking with God on the Road You Never Wanted to Travel

"Hurting people need more than a pat on the back and a few stale clichés, and they get it in *Walking with God on the Road You Never Wanted to Travel*. With all the warmth, insight, and splashes of humor we've come to expect, Mark Atteberry offers biblical, workable strategies for negotiating the hard roads of life. This is one of those rare books that rings so true, it makes you wonder why someone didn't write it a long time ago."

—Barbara Johnson
Best-selling author of *Laughter
from Heaven* and *Stick a
Geranium in Your Hat and Be
Happy*

"If the circumstances of your life have grown so difficult that you honestly don't know what to do, take heart. *Walking with God on the Road You Never Wanted to Travel* was written just for you."

—Angela Thomas
Best-selling Author of *Do You
Think I'm Beautiful?* and *A
Beautiful Offering*

"Mark has brought us a chronicle of pain, discovery, and ultimate peace. I found myself on the pages of his inspired perspective."

—Janet Paschal
Grammy and Dove Award
Nominated Singer/Songwriter

Other Books by Mark Atteberry

The Caleb Quest

The Samson Syndrome

The Climb of Your Life

Walking with God on the Road You **Never** Wanted to Travel

Mark Atteberry

NELSON BOOKS
A Division of Thomas Nelson Publishers
Since 1798

www.thomasnelson.com

Published in Nashville, Tennessee, by Thomas Nelson, Inc.

Author is represented by the literary agency of Alive Communications, Inc., 7680 Goddard Street, Suite 200, Colorado Springs, CO 80920.

Nelson Books titles may be purchased in bulk for educational, business, fund-raising, or sales promotional use. For information, please e-mail SpecialMarkets@ThomasNelson.com.

Unless otherwise noted, Scripture quotations are from the *Holy Bible,* New Living Translation, copyright © 1996. Used by permission of Tyndale House Publishers, Inc., Wheaton, Illinois 60189. All rights reserved.

Scripture quotations noted NIV are from the HOLY BIBLE, NEW INTERNATIONAL VERSION®. Copyright © 1973, 1978, 1984 by International Bible Society. Used by permission of Zondervan Publishing House. All rights reserved.

Scripture quotations noted KJV are from the KING JAMES VERSION of the Holy Bible.

Library of Congress Cataloging-in-Publication Data

Atteberry, Mark.
    Walking with God on the road you never wanted to travel / by Mark Atteberry.
        p. cm.
    Includes bibliographical references.
    ISBN-10 0-7852-1132-2 (pbk.)
    ISBN-13 978-0-7852-1132-7 (pbk.)
        1. Consolation. 2. Exodus, The. 3. Wilderness (Theology) I. Title.
BV4905.3.A86 2005
248.8'6—dc22   2005008733

Printed in the United States of America

07 08 RRD 5 4

For Mary Berlin

On the day I finished this manuscript, Mary had her left leg ampu-
tated. It was her twelfth major surgery in the last eight years. As her
pastor, I've spent countless hours visiting her in various hospitals,
nursing homes, and rehab centers and have never heard her utter a
word of complaint. Her unshakable faith was a constant source of
inspiration to me during the year I spent writing this book. Because
of her, no one will ever be able to say the strategies presented here are
too difficult to accomplish. Mary mastered them all.

CONTENTS

Introduction   ix

Author's Note   xv

Strategy #1   1
Understand How You Wound Up in the Wilderness

Strategy #2   15
Commit to Strict Obedience

Strategy #3   27
Travel with a Friend

Strategy #4   41
Stay Positive

Strategy #5   55
Step over the Dead and Keep Going

Strategy #6   71
Trust God to Meet Your Needs

Strategy #7   85
Go at God's Pace

CONTENTS

Strategy #8   97
Enjoy Every Oasis

Strategy #9   113
Expect Detours

Strategy #10   127
Worship on the Way

Strategy #11   143
Keep Your Dreams Alive

Strategy #12   157
When You Come to the Jordan, Cross It

Strategy #13   171
Turn Your Trip into a Testimony

A Letter from Mark   183

Study Guide   185

About the Author   199

Acknowledgments   201

Notes   203

Anna Hartman walked into our church every Sunday with her husband and two small boys, passing out kisses and hugs like Christmas candy. It didn't matter if she knew you or not. If you were in her path, you got one or the other. Or both. And there was nothing fake about it. Anna was the genuine article: a committed, joy-filled, low-maintenance Christian.

One day her doctor told her she needed a tonsillectomy. He assured her it was nothing to worry about—just a couple of little snips. She'd be in the hospital overnight and then go home and eat ice cream for a day or two. Her plan was to lay in a supply of Ben & Jerry's and enjoy the time off work.

But on the morning after the surgery, Anna was running a slight fever. The doctor seemed puzzled, but not alarmed. "It happens sometimes," he said. "Just plan to stay one more night, and we'll try to have you out of here by noon tomorrow." Anna was disappointed but figured one more night in the hospital wouldn't be the end of the world.

She was wrong.

Late that night, as she lay alone in her room, an artery ruptured in her throat and produced an outpouring of blood so excessive that it choked and drowned her in a matter of minutes. The remote-control device that she could have used to call for help was found dangling from her bed. No doubt she'd been groping frantically for it during her last seconds of life.

When the nurse found her, Anna had been dead for some time. Her gown and bed linens were soaked in blood. Pools were congealing on the floor. Streaks and splatters were head-high on the walls and privacy curtain. The room looked like a scene from a bad horror film.

The doctor who performed the surgery was called and arrived in no time. I was sitting in the waiting room with Anna's husband, Ron, when he came in to express his sympathy. "It was an act of God," he explained. "One of those freaky things that no one could have predicted."

But it wasn't that simple.

An autopsy revealed that an artery had been nicked during the tonsillectomy. The pathologist called it a ticking bomb just waiting to explode. And explode it did.

I sat with Ron while Anna's body was removed, and then we walked out to our cars. I'll never forget the conversation we had there in the light of a street lamp at about 1:00 a.m.

"Mark, why did God let this happen?"

"I don't know, Ron."

"We prayed for her."

"I know."

"All of us. Me, you, and the boys. We stood in a circle and held hands and asked God to protect her."

"I know."

"So why didn't He?"

"I honestly don't know, Ron. I wish I did."

"It all seems like some kind of cruel joke. I mean, she was only twenty-eight!"

"I know."

Ron fell silent for a moment and stared off into space. I knew that images of his beloved Anna had to be flashing through his mind.

Their first date.

Their wedding day.

The births of their children.

The last time they made love.

Even in the dim light, I could see that Ron's cheeks were wet with tears. He stared off into the starry night and then turned to me and said in a trembling voice, "This is my worst nightmare. I have no idea how I'm going to get through this."

I could have put my hand on his shoulder and said, "Just trust the Lord, Ron. He'll take care of you." But I knew he would counter with the observation that the Lord hadn't done a very good job of taking care of Anna. And quite honestly, that was an issue I didn't feel up to addressing.

So I said nothing.

That night, through no fault of his own, Ron Hartman suddenly found himself on a very hard road, one that he never wanted to travel. Sadly, the road proved a little too steep and treacherous. In an apparent attempt to find some relief from the loneliness and painful memories, he remarried quickly and moved far away. That was several years ago. The last I heard, he was struggling mightily.

I wish I could say that Ron's case is rare and isolated, but it isn't. Every day, people from all walks of life suddenly find themselves on roads they never wanted to travel:

"It's malignant."

"I've found someone else."

"I don't love you anymore."

"Your son has been arrested."

"Mom, I think I'm pregnant."

"You may never walk again."

"Your wife didn't survive the surgery."

"There's been a shooting at your son's school."

These are just a few of the statements that can jerk you off the smooth, flat pavement of your well-ordered life and send you careening down a blind alley or, worse yet, to the crumbling edge of a dangerous mountain cliff. The noxious mixture of shock, anger, and grief, along with the unanswerable questions these statements produce, can set your head spinning. Like my friend Ron, you can suddenly find yourself spiritually disoriented and making harmful choices that will haunt you forever. Or, like countless other people, you can simply give up hope and join the ranks of the living dead.

As a pastor, I know all too well that the hard roads of life are littered with the souls of good people who found them too hard to negotiate. Even now, as I'm writing these words, faces are flashing through my mind. The faces of people I've loved and laughed with and worshipped with. Good people who touched my life in special ways but never will again because they died or got lost on roads they would never have chosen in a million years.

Are you on a hard road right now? Have you recently had your world rocked by one of the bombshell statements listed above? Are you reeling from the shock? Boiling with anger? So heartbroken and confused that you don't know what to do? If so, I'm glad God saw fit to bring you and this book together. What you have in your hands is a road map of sorts, a traveler's guide for the hard roads of life.

I found this road map tucked away in my Bible. No, it wasn't a dog-eared piece of paper with directional signs and navigational symbols. It was a Bible story. The story of a group of people who once traveled the hardest road of all. Yes, I'm referring to the story of the Israelites, *God's* people, and their forty-year trek through the wilderness. It was an arduous journey through a dark and dangerous land. There were setbacks, detours, and losses along the way. Heavy losses, as we will see. But the story has a happy ending. With God's help, they found their way safely back to the land flowing with milk and honey.

What I've discovered is that their story contains timeless lessons that apply with uncanny relevance to the hard-road journeys that modern believers are called upon to make. I've turned these into thirteen strategies. They're so simple that even a child can understand them, yet they're so powerful that any one of them could save your life. Taken as a group, they are a map you can follow. They are a light for your path. They are a reason for hope.

Earlier, I mentioned my silence in response to Ron Hartman's agony on that terrible night when his wife died so unexpectedly. At the time, I felt that my inability to say something profound was an indictment of sorts. I remember feeling ashamed as I drove home in the wee hours of the morning. I now realize that I was making a simple but common mistake. I was looking for a way to explain *why* such terrible things were happening to him, when I should have simply offered a few ideas on *how* he could face the future. You see, the *whys* of life are often out of our reach. I'm convinced that only eternity will unlock all of their mysteries. But the *hows* are a different story. The Bible is chock-full of *hows*.

For the most part, this is a book of *hows*, not *whys*. I'll leave the philosophers to argue the whys of life. My goal is simply to share the wonderful news I've discovered—that even the hardest roads lead home.

Come. Let me show you.

The epic story of the Israelites' forty-year trek through the wilderness is one of the richest and most challenging in the Bible. It's told in the books of Exodus, Leviticus, Numbers, Deuteronomy, and Joshua, yet many intriguing references to it pop up throughout Scripture. As you read, it will help you to remember that I have made no attempt to address everything that happened during those forty years. Nor have I necessarily arranged the events in chronological order. In other words, this book more resembles a slide presentation than a movie. I've assembled thirteen photographs, taken along that hardest of roads, that I believe will speak in a powerful way to hard-road travelers today.

Also, I tell many stories about real people in this book, but in order to protect their privacy, I have changed some names and altered a few minor details.

Because you complained against me, none of you who are twenty years old or older and were counted in the census will enter the land I swore to give you. The only exceptions will be Caleb son of Jephunneh and Joshua son of Nun.

You said your children would be taken captive. Well, I will bring them safely into the land, and they will enjoy what you have despised. But as for you, your dead bodies will fall in this wilderness. And your children will be like shepherds, wandering in the wilderness forty years. In this way, they will pay for your faithlessness, until the last of you lies dead in the wilderness.

—NUMBERS 14:29–33

Understand How You
Wound Up in the Wilderness

You will know the truth, and the truth will set you free.
—JESUS, IN JOHN 8:32

The fact that you have picked up this book and begun to read tells me that you're probably on a hard road you never wanted to travel.

Maybe you're sitting in a house made silent by the departure of your spouse.

Maybe you're lying in a hospital bed with an eight-inch scar in your chest.

Maybe you've just been threatened by an angry creditor.

Or maybe your boss recently handed you a pink slip.

Right off the bat, I'm going to ask you to do something that might be a little painful. Okay, it might be *extremely* painful. But it's a critical exercise—one that lays the foundation for all the strategies to come. It's a step you simply cannot skip if you want to get through your wilderness in good mental and spiritual health.

I want you to take your eyes off the road ahead, do an about-face, and look at your back trail. I know you're worried about the future. You're wondering where this awful road is going to take you and what monsters might be hiding along the way. That's understandable, and we'll get to that. But for the next few minutes, I want you to forget where you're going and think about where you've been. In this first chapter, the goal is to answer one question: How did you get where you are?

In Psalm 77:5–6, Asaph said, "I think of the good old days, long since ended, when my nights were filled with joyful songs. I search my soul and think about the difference now." Some people would say that such reflection is pointless. After all, what's done is done; you can't change the past. Yet, Solomon said, "Wisdom is enshrined in an understanding heart" (Prov. 14:33). He also said, "People who cherish understanding will prosper" (Prov. 19:8). Our goal in this chapter is simply to gain understanding. Resolving the issue of how you wound up in the wilderness could help you in three ways.

First, it could point you toward the way of escape. Many times the road *into* the wilderness is also the road *out*. For example, if a destructive behavior pattern has broken one of your relationships, correcting that behavior will likely be the key to its healing. Or, if reckless spending habits have put you deep into debt, fiscal self-discipline is the only thing that will get you out and keep you out. Problems and solutions are often found at opposite ends of the same road.

Second, understanding how you wound up in the wilderness could keep you from making the same mistake again. I know a woman who's been married and divorced three times. She likes to tell everybody that she's "unlucky in love," but unlucky is not how I would describe her. I'd say she just hasn't been paying attention. She hasn't learned her lessons. Every time she finds her way out of the wilderness, she unwittingly turns around and marches right back in!

And third, understanding how you wound up in the wilderness could lift a load of guilt off your shoulders. What if it suddenly dawned on you that none of the mess you're in was your fault? What if you suddenly realized that you could have done nothing to prevent it? Such a realization wouldn't make your hard road any shorter, but it would make it a little easier by lightening the load you're carrying. No burden is heavier—and thus sweeter to get rid of—than guilt.

For all of these reasons, I encourage you to take the next few minutes and look at your recent history. After thinking honestly about how you got where you are, you should be able to settle on one of three possibilities.

It Was Your Fault

The Israelites spent much of their wilderness time bellyaching. More than anything, they hated the monotony. They hated eating the same food every single day. They hated having to repeatedly set up and tear down their tents. They hated having to pack up and lug their stuff from one desolate place to another. But more than anything, they hated the feeling that they were going nowhere. Day after day, week after week, month after month, and year after year, they trudged across a landscape that never seemed to change. No wonder they were always cranky!

But they had nobody to blame but themselves.

They could have avoided the wilderness simply by obeying the Lord's instructions to take possession of the land of Canaan. God had promised to give them the land. He had brought them safely out of Egypt, where they'd been living as slaves, and led them straight to its doorstep. And He had assured them that He would help them defeat the pagan tribes that lived there if they would only trust Him. But when the spies who were sent in to reconnoiter the land brought back reports of giants and fortified cities, the people became afraid:

All the people began weeping aloud, and they cried all night. Their voices rose in a great chorus of complaint against Moses and Aaron. "We wish we had died in Egypt, or even here in the wilderness!" they wailed. Why is the LORD taking us to this country only to have us die in battle? Our wives and little ones will be carried off as slaves! Let's get out of here and return to Egypt!" Then they plotted among themselves, "Let's choose a leader and go back to Egypt!" (Num. 14:1–4)

God was offended by this attitude, especially since He had gone to such great lengths to liberate them. He had done for them what they could never have done for themselves, even drowning the entire Egyptian army in the waters of the Red Sea as a glorious demonstration of His supreme authority over every human enemy. But their memories of that great miracle were clouded by frightening reports of giant warriors and walled cities. They panicked, pure and simple, and it made God angry.

Of course, God could have wiped them out altogether. In fact, that was His initial thought (Num. 14:12). But after Moses interceded on their behalf, God changed His mind. He decided that if the people didn't want the beautiful and bountiful land He was prepared to give them, they could have the wilderness. And they could have it for the next forty years . . . until every faithless, complaining person in the entire nation was dead and buried (Num. 14:29–30).

I don't know if God was ever angrier than He was at that time. In fact, I've always felt that Numbers 14:34 contains the most chilling statement God ever made to His people: "You will discover what it is like to have me for an enemy."

Clearly, the Israelites had no one but themselves to blame for their predicament. And so it is with a lot of people today who are dragging themselves along the hard roads of life.

Kobe Bryant would be a case in point.

At this point, it looks as though only he and his young female accuser will ever know if he really sexually assaulted her. But whether he did or didn't, it can't be disputed that he alone is responsible for the trashing of his reputation. While traveling without his wife, he invited a young hotel employee to his room late at night and, at the very least, committed adultery. Talk about inviting trouble! If he'd studied for a year, I doubt that he could have come up with a dumber idea.

Or what about Dave Bliss, the recently disgraced basketball coach at Baylor University? After the mysterious death of one of his players, Bliss was secretly recorded encouraging several people associated with the basketball program to portray the deceased player as a drug dealer, knowing full well there was no evidence to support such a claim. It was a brainless, desperate attempt to divert attention away from unethical conduct within the Baylor basketball program, and it cost him both his career and his reputation.

Recently, I ran across this quote: "One of the annoying things about believing in free will and personal responsibility is the difficulty of finding someone to blame your problems on. And when you do find somebody, it's remarkable how often his picture turns up on your driver's license."

If you pulled your driver's license out right now, would you be staring at the mug shot of the person who got you into trouble? If so, you need to admit it. As painful and humiliating as it might be, you need to own up to your mistakes and commit yourself to never making them again. Proverbs 28:13 says, "People who cover over their sins will not prosper. But if they confess and forsake them, they will receive mercy."

But of course, there is a second possibility . . .

It Was Somebody Else's Fault

Caleb and Joshua were two of the original twelve spies that were sent into the land of Canaan. They, too, saw the giants and the well-fortified cities. But unlike their ten companions, they believed the giants and the cities would be no match for God. Brimming with faith, they begged their countrymen to follow God's instructions. They pleaded with them to move forward in obedience and trust the One who had never failed to protect them. But it was to no avail. They were outvoted and almost stoned for daring to stand against the majority (Num. 14:10).

I can only imagine what a bitter pill Israel's sentence must have been for Caleb and Joshua. They had done nothing wrong. They bore not an ounce of guilt. Yet, there they were, loading up their gear and striking out for the wilderness as if they were as bad as everybody else. What an injustice! Two great heroes of the faith had to put all of their hopes and dreams on hold for forty long years because of other people's sins.

Can you relate?

Are you on a hard road right now through no fault of your own?

Let me caution you to tap the brakes right here and not answer this question too hastily. We all have a natural tendency to blame our problems on others. Recently, an overweight man filed a lawsuit against McDonald's, Wendy's, Burger King, and KFC, alleging that their food made him fat. He was right, of course. The problem is, nobody held a gun to his head and made him eat it. That's basically what the judge said when he ruled against the man.

Frivolous lawsuits are rampant today, which illustrates the difficulty a lot of people have when it comes to accepting responsibility for their actions. We are so desperate to feel good about ourselves that we have turned buck-passing into an art form.

Please don't do that. Don't blame somebody else for a problem you created . . . or that you could have prevented.

On the other hand, if someone else really is to blame for your situation, now is the time to say so. Not out loud, necessarily. You don't have to shout it from the rooftops or take out an ad in the paper. In fact, nobody else even needs to know. The point here is not to seek revenge or send your antagonist on a guilt trip. The point is simply to let *yourself* off the hook. You need to get to the place where you're not beating yourself up over what happened.

I know that last paragraph will cause some of my readers to bristle. When you've been hurt and you know who the perpetrator is, you naturally want to shout it from the rooftops. You feel it's your duty. You tell yourself that justice demands it, that you're only protecting other potential victims, or that you would be sacrificing your self-respect if you failed to stand up and fight back.

But wait!

Remember why you're reading this book: You're trying to get through the wilderness. You're trying to find your way to the end of a long, hard road.

When you focus on your enemy, you undermine that goal. How? By distracting yourself from your true purpose and by expending valuable energy on a pursuit that does nothing to advance your cause. Believe me, if the road you're facing looks so scary or difficult that you decided to pick up this book and read it, then you can't afford to waste even one ounce of energy. You're going to have to focus completely on the principles in this book and jettison every single distraction if you hope to make it through.

Read the next sentence slowly and let it soak in: *People who seek revenge are the ones who die on this road.*

Trust me on this.

I've been a pastor for a long time and I've seen it happen. People commit spiritual suicide trying to settle old scores. I've watched them do it even while pleading with them to stop. Hebrews 12:15 says, "Watch out that no bitter root of unbelief rises up among you, for whenever it springs up, *many are corrupted by its poison*" (emphasis added). Have you ever read that verse and wondered what the "bitter root of unbelief" is? I believe it's the anger and resentment that cause you to abandon everything you used to believe about love and forgiveness. It's the boiling, gurgling bitterness that corrupts your soul like poison.

Cutting out that "bitter root"—forgiving the person who put you on this road—may be the hardest challenge you'll face in this book . . . and the most important. In fact, if you're struggling with anger and animosity, I'd suggest that you not move ahead to Chapter 2 until you get that bitter root cut out. Nothing you'll read in the rest of this book will help you in any appreciable way if you continue to harbor bitterness in your heart. Forgiveness always has been (and always will be) a prerequisite to healing and restoration.

Let me offer two facts that might make it easier for you to pick up your ax and start chopping at that bitter root.

First, remember that when you choose to hold a grudge, you make yourself a prisoner. This was illustrated in the life of a man I knew years ago. When his wife left him for another man, he vowed that he would never give them a moment's peace. He left messages on their answering machine, wrote angry letters, and followed them around, often popping up out of nowhere and embarrassing them in public. One day he completely lost control and began pounding on the door and screaming profanity-laced threats. Frightened, she called the police and he was arrested.

It wasn't until he found himself staring through the bars of a jail cell for the first time in his life that the reality hit him: He'd become

UNDERSTAND HOW YOU WOUND UP IN THE WILDERNESS

a prisoner. Not just in the physical sense but, even more important, in the spiritual sense. He'd become a prisoner of hate.

My friend, hate is a terrible taskmaster. It will beat you senseless. It will have you doing things that are beyond stupid. And it will laugh in your face when you get caught and have to pay the price. Honestly, I've never met a grudge holder who wasn't miserable. They don't all get thrown into jail like the man I just referred to, but every revenge seeker I've ever known has been tormented and unhappy.

You will not be the exception.

The second fact I want you to remember is that God has promised to settle all your old scores. Romans 12:17–19 says, "Never pay back evil for evil to anyone. Do things in such a way that everyone can see you are honorable. Do your part to live in peace with everyone, as much as possible. Dear friends, never avenge yourselves. Leave that to God. For it is written, 'I will take vengeance; I will repay those who deserve it' says the Lord."

Here Paul makes it clear that when you leave the paybacks to God, it doesn't mean your antagonist is getting away with anything. In fact, I'm confident that any action God might take against your opponent would be more fitting (and probably more unpleasant) than anything you could dream up. When you grant forgiveness, you're simply stepping aside and allowing God to handle the situation so you can concentrate on more important matters.

Like getting home safely.

It Was Nobody's Fault

This is the third possibility you need to consider as you think about how you wound up in the wilderness.

Those of us who live in Florida are used to visitors. But never have we had one that stirred things up like Andrew. Hurricane Andrew, that is. He arrived kicking and screaming in August of 1992. He stayed only a few hours, but while he was here he killed twenty-three people and caused $26.5 billion in damage, making him the costliest natural disaster in U.S. history.

Three months later I drove through Homestead, Florida, which bore the brunt of the storm. I got a lump in my throat as I surveyed the devastation caused by Andrew's 160-miles-per-hour winds. Entire neighborhoods were wiped off the face of the earth. Countless homes and businesses were turned into toothpicks. Many homeowners had used spray paint to write messages on what was left of their houses. Most wrote their insurance policy numbers and phone numbers where they could be reached. But a few used the opportunity to vent their feelings. I'll never forget one message that was scrawled across the only standing wall of what had been a modest, wood-frame home. It simply said: "Damn you, Andrew!"

The owner of that house expressed a sentiment that I'm sure tens of thousands of people felt. And perhaps the expression made him feel a little better. But in truth, no one was to blame for the devastation. We give our storms human names, but they are not human. They have no will and they cannot reason. They just happen, and there's nothing anybody can do to prevent them. The damage and suffering they cause is nobody's fault.

When I sat down to outline this chapter and identified the three possibilities I wanted to talk about, I knew this third one—"It was nobody's fault"—would be a tough one to deal with. Why? Because experience has taught me that when people can't find a human being to blame their struggles on, God becomes a suspect.

Back when Hurricane Andrew left a trail of death and destruction through our state, I was bombarded with questions:

"Do you think this was God's judgment?"

"Do you think this was a wake-up call from God?"

"Do you think God is angry?"

The same thing happens every time there's a major earthquake or flood or epidemic. I remember when the SARS epidemic was picking up a head of steam and headlining the news on a nightly basis, there was a lot of talk among believers about God being fed up and ready to teach this world a lesson. Then a cure was found and the talk suddenly died out.

I don't pretend to know the mind of God. His thoughts are far too majestic for my little brain to grasp. But I do feel uneasy when I hear people blaming Him for every unhappy turn of events. Have we forgotten that we live in a fallen, sin-corrupted world?

Instead of blaming God, stop and imagine what life would be like if we didn't have His Word, His Spirit, His angels, or His church. The assistance He provides through these channels is invaluable. Without these gifts, we would be completely helpless. Sure, we have suffered, but who can say how much suffering we've been spared? Who can calculate the number of times God has intervened on our behalf? Who can say if you or I would even be alive today if not for God's protection?

One night several years ago, my wife Marilyn and I were awakened by an urgent pounding at our front door. I stumbled out of bed and looked out the window, wondering who on earth it could be. When I saw a vehicle that belonged to a young man my daughter worked with, I felt my heart sink. I glanced at my watch and saw that it was a few minutes after eleven. She'd just gotten off work. Somehow, I knew she'd been in an accident.

Sure enough, not two miles from home, she'd lost control of her car and crashed into a tree. When Marilyn and I arrived, emergency vehicles with flashing lights were already on the scene, and Michelle was lying on a stretcher. She was already in a neck brace, and paramedics were working diligently. My only child. I honestly thought I might be sick.

As it turned out, she was taken to the hospital, treated, and released with minor injuries.

What amazed me was the way her car had struck the tree. Because she'd been traveling at least 50 miles per hour, the impact was horrific. The authorities told us there was only one way the car could have hit the tree without causing the driver serious injuries and possible death. That way was broadside, with the passenger door taking the impact. In order to hit the tree that way, the car had to spin 180 degrees (because the tree was on her left) and the timing had to be split-second perfect.

It did, and it was.

I often think back to that night and wonder if God was responsible for spinning that car around. Many would laugh at the notion and insist it happened by chance. Others would be happy to blame God for not preventing the accident. But my heart told me then—and still does—that He protected her.

In Jeremiah 29:11 God says, "I know the plans I have for you . . . They are plans for good and not for disaster, to give you a future and a hope." That verse, along with countless others, simply will not allow me to picture God as a temperamental bully who beats His children. I cannot imagine Him toying with us, inflicting pain and suffering just because He can. Yes, I know that He occasionally disciplines His children and that His disciplinary actions can be very painful. The wilderness journey of the Israelites is the ultimate example. But even when He takes such measures, His motivation is love and His desire is to make a better future for His people (Heb. 12:11–13).

If you're on a hard road that you never wanted to travel, I would encourage you to think long and hard before you point an accusing finger at God. You're going to need Him if you hope to make it through. The last thing you want to do is shut Him out of your life. Remember, sometimes trouble is nobody's fault.

I hope this review of your recent past has given you a clearer understanding of what you need to do in order to move forward in a positive way. You may need to repent, or at least reform some aspect of your behavior to keep from compounding your troubles. You may need to forgive someone who mistreated you. Or you may need to apologize to God for casting blame in His direction and accept that no one is to blame.

Any one of these steps will give you the closure you need and set you in the proper frame of mind to move forward. There are many steps ahead of you. They'll be easier if there's nothing deadly stalking you from behind.

These events happened as a warning to us, so that we would not crave evil things as they did or worship idols as some of them did. For the Scriptures say, "The people celebrated with feasting and drinking, and they indulged themselves in pagan revelry." And we must not engage in sexual immorality as some of them did, causing 23,000 of them to die in one day. Nor should we put Christ to the test, as some of them did and then died from snakebites. And don't grumble as some of them did, for that is why God sent his angel of death to destroy them. All these events happened to them as examples for us. They were written down to warn us, who live at the time when this age is drawing to a close. If you think you are standing strong, be careful, for you, too, may fall into the same sin.

—1 Corinthians 10:6–12

Who made God angry for forty years? Wasn't it the people who sinned, whose bodies fell in the wilderness? And to whom was God speaking when he vowed that they would never enter his place of rest? He was speaking to those who disobeyed him.

—Hebrews 3:17–18

Commit to Strict Obedience

Make me walk along the path of your commands,
for that is where my happiness is found.

—PSALM 119:35

Marie was an attractive, outgoing woman who gave every indication of being a super wife and mother. But for some reason, her husband packed up and left. As far as she could tell, there wasn't another woman in his life. He simply grew tired of what he called "the daily grind of being married." He said he needed his freedom, and he was gone less than six hours after dropping the bomb.

Just that quickly, Marie found herself on a road she never wanted to travel. And because she didn't see it coming, her devastation was complete. It took lots of counseling and tons of loving support from her friends to get her through those dark days. But in time, she started smiling again and appeared to be doing very well.

Of course, appearances can be deceiving.

One morning, she stopped by my office. I could tell something was wrong. She wore no makeup, which was unusual. Her hair and clothes were a mess, her eyes were bloodshot, and her hands were shaking almost uncontrollably. I'd never seen her in such a state. But when she told me her story, it all made sense.

Shortly after her husband left, an unbelieving coworker talked her into going out on the town. "You can't just sit around and lick your wounds," she'd said. "You need to get out and have some fun. Meet some new people. Show that husband of yours that he can't ruin your life."

Marie had never been into the bar scene, but it didn't take her long to get into it. The party atmosphere made her feel alive. The music was loud, the men were good looking, and the conversations were sufficiently shallow. It had been years since guys had openly flirted with her, and she couldn't believe how good it felt. A single suggestive remark or a pair of handsome eyes roaming appreciatively over her body made her feel almost euphoric. She told herself it was therapeutic, just a little harmless fun. Nevertheless, she hid the fact from her Christian friends. Somehow, she knew they wouldn't understand.

In no time, Marie had a double life going. She still went to church and associated with her Christian friends, but one or two nights a week she was out partying. She'd never been a drinker, but with guys constantly offering to buy them for her, it was easy to start. She liked the buzz it gave her. Everything seemed more fun after she'd had a couple of drinks.

And then it happened.

One morning, she woke up in bed with a man whose name she didn't know. It happened to be her own bed, which meant that she'd brought the stranger to her home—something she had sworn she'd never do. She couldn't remember inviting him. She also couldn't remember having sex, though it was obvious she had. Suddenly, a thousand terrifying possibilities were swirling in her head. It was easily the most frightening moment of her life.

I was very sad to hear about Marie's poor choices, but I wasn't totally surprised. Hard-road travelers have always been some of Satan's favorite targets.

When I was a kid, my whole family loved to fish. My brothers and I would load up all of our poles and tackle boxes, and when Mom and Dad got off work, we would head for the country. Because it was a rural area, there were farm ponds everywhere. We literally had dozens to choose from. But we always wound up at the same two or three places because, over time, they had produced the most fish.

Satan is no different. He, too, is fishing. Not for fish, but for the souls of men. And he's been around long enough to know where the good fishing is. Without question, his favorite "fishing hole" would be any hard road . . . any set of circumstances where people are in pain. He understands the vulnerability. He recognizes that people in pain will often grope for anything that holds the promise of relief, even if it's temporary. It's the perfect setup for his lies, his shiny little lures that have the razor-sharp treble hooks hidden in them.

We can certainly see this in the wilderness journey of the Israelites. Satan dogged their steps and worked tirelessly during that forty-year period, because he knew their pain, their fatigue, and their obvious desire for relief would weaken their resolve. Were his efforts successful? Read these two verses and judge for yourself:

> Oh, how often they rebelled against him in the desert and grieved his heart in the wilderness. Again and again they tested God's patience and frustrated the Holy One of Israel. (Ps. 78:40–41)

Oh yes, Satan found the fishing to be very good during those years. He enticed the Israelites into a wide variety of detestable sins, everything from grumbling and complaining (Num. 21:4–5), to having sex with pagan tribes (Num. 25:1), to worshipping false gods (Num. 25:2–3).

When hard-road travelers come to my office looking for help, I never let them get away without encouraging them to be very careful with their lifestyle choices. I try not to scare them, but I do want them to understand that Satan is lurking along the hard roads of this world, licking his chops, just waiting for some hurting person to come limping along. There are two truths I try to underscore.

Strict Obedience Will Straighten Your Road

Poinciana Christian Church, where I have preached since 1989, has facilities on Pleasant Hill Road in Osceola County, Florida. I've never quite understood how the road got its name. For one thing, there's not a hill for miles around. Also, when the road was first built, there was nothing pleasant about it. Now it's a beautiful four-lane highway, but when I first arrived in the area it was a narrow, winding, two-lane death trap. In fact, the locals dubbed it "Pleasant Kill Road" because of the number of fatalities it produced.

When Pleasant Hill Road was rebuilt in the late nineties, straightening it was one of the top priorities. There are still a few long, lazy curves, but those of the sharp, hairpin variety are long gone. And so is much of the danger. No one ever calls it Pleasant Kill Road anymore.

No road is completely safe, but everybody knows that crooked, winding roads hold an extra element of danger. And it's true even in the spiritual realm. Solomon said, "People with integrity have firm footing, but those who follow crooked paths will slip and fall" (Prov. 10:9).

I can't read those words without thinking about Marie, whom I mentioned at the beginning of this chapter. She was already on a hard road, one that was going to present greater challenges than any she'd faced before. But those challenges were multiplied when she started following a crooked path. She handled them for a while, and even enjoyed the thrill. (Crooked roads can be a lot of fun, as any sports car owner knows!) But on the terrible night I described to you, that crooked road became her undoing. Spiritually speaking, she was moving a little too fast and came to a curve that was a little too sharp.

Dear reader, if the road you're following right now is a hard one, you probably can't change that. But you can make sure it's a straight one. It makes no sense to add an extra measure of danger to the challenges you're already facing.

Here's some good advice:

Look straight ahead, and fix your eyes on what lies before you. *Mark out a straight path for your feet; then stick to the path and stay safe.* Don't get sidetracked; keep your feet from following evil. (Prov. 4:25–27, emphasis added)

You might want to type up those words and put them where you'll see them every day. They'll remind you that you have two important responsibilities.

First, it's your responsibility to mark out a straight path for your feet. It's not the responsibility of your pastor or your parents or your spouse. It's yours. *You're* the one who has to pick up *your* Bible and figure out where God wants *you* to walk.

The good news is, it's not that difficult.

The Bible is a big, fat book with tiny print. It can look intimidating just sitting on a coffee table. But contrary to what most people believe, God's instructions are very forthright and uncomplicated. The Ten Commandments, for example, are simple enough that even children can read and understand them. And the words of Jesus in the Sermon on the Mount (Matt. 5–7) are striking in their simplicity. You can also refer to study guides or seek the help of an older, wiser Christian. Just going to church and listening to a good sermon every week will help you mark out a straight path for your feet. I could go on. My point is not that you'll never be puzzled by anything you read in the Bible. It's simply that the important stuff is hard to miss and often easy to understand.

Second, once you've marked out that straight path, it's your responsibility to stick to it. This, of course, is the hard part.

When I was a teenager, our family vacation took us through the Badlands of South Dakota, which is one of the creepiest places I've ever visited. It's a surreal, lunarlike landscape. It's nothing but sandstone buttes and craggy fingers of rock as far as the eye can see. Early French trappers referred to the region as *"les mauvaises terres a terverser,"* which means, "a bad land to travel through." Perceptive, those trappers!

I remember Dad pulling into a rest area where we got out to stretch our legs and snap a few pictures. The place was a little unsettling because of the signs that were posted everywhere: "Danger! Rattlesnakes! Stay on sidewalk!" But did people obey? Of course not. They meandered here and there, collecting rocks or looking for the perfect photo op, as if the signs didn't exist.

That's people for you.

We can look right at a warning and ignore it, whether it's a Stay on the Sidewalk sign or one of the Ten Commandments. Of course, this is what Satan is banking on. He's counting on you to ignore the simple commands of God that you've read in the Bible. He's hoping the pain of your hard road will make you so hungry for pleasure that you'll be willing to step away from the straight path you've marked out, even if only for a moment. You see, all he needs is an instant. Many a devastating sin has been committed on impulse. Even one step to the right or left of righteousness could bring disastrous results.

My friend, don't take that step. Don't ignore God's warnings and go meandering into forbidden territory. It'll only make your hard road harder. Instead, commit to strict obedience. Be like David, who said, "The wicked have set their traps for me along your path, but I will not turn from your commandments" (Ps. 119:110). Strict obedience will straighten your road.

But that's not all . . .

Strict Obedience Will Lighten Your Load

You've heard of Murphy's Law. It's the idea that if something can go wrong, it will. Well, let me tell you about another law. I don't know if it's ever been formally named, but as sure as God is in heaven, it's true. Here it is: Junk accumulates.

If you doubt the veracity of this law, just go look in your garage. Or your bedroom closet. Or your desk drawer. Or better yet, under the front seat of your car. Under the front seat of the typical American's car you can find an old road map, an umbrella, more than a dollar in change, an empty fast-food wrapper, two wadded-up tissues, and enough French fries to feed a family of five for a week.

Believe me, junk accumulates.

A couple of years ago Marilyn and I moved out of a home we had lived in for eleven years. From the amount of junk we got rid of, you would have thought we had lived there for fifty years. I'm not kidding when I say that we found stuff we didn't even know we owned. Marilyn would hold something up and say, "Where did we get this?" And I would answer, "I don't know. I've never seen it before." I began to suspect that people were bringing stuff into our house when we weren't home. Or that perhaps our daughter had opened a storage business on the side without telling us. Then I realized that it was just that eternal (and infernal) law at work.

Junk accumulates.

And it doesn't just accumulate in our garages and attics and closets and underneath our car seats. It also accumulates in our lives. In our minds and our hearts. I'm talking about worries and burdens and fears and frustrations. That's one of the reasons why it feels so good to go to church on Sunday. There's something about being with Christian friends, singing uplifting songs, sharing in the Lord's Supper, and hearing the Word preached that helps us dump all that stuff, at least for a while. I know there have been a thousand occasions when I walked into church on Sunday morning feeling burdened and tired in my faith and left a couple of hours later feeling refreshed and rejuvenated. In Psalm 81:6 God said, "I will relieve your shoulder of its burden; I will free your hands from their heavy tasks." Even God acknowledges that junk accumulates in our lives. Now, here's the good news.

Yes, junk accumulates, but you have control over the rate of accumulation! You can avoid a lot of *unnecessary* burdens simply by committing to strict obedience.

Korah's rebellion is a perfect illustration.

The shocking story, told in Numbers 16, is one of the most tragic to emerge from the wilderness years. It all started when a troublemaker named Korah decided that he'd like to have Moses' job. He was a power-hungry egomaniac who believed that he could get Moses thrown out of office if he could find enough influential people who would stand behind him. A show of force, he thought, would pressure Moses into resigning. So, with the help of a couple of his buddies, he began a secret recruitment drive. I picture him sneaking around after dark, slipping in and out of the tents of some of Moses' more outspoken critics. I can just imagine him feeding their frustrations and talking about how much better all of their lives would be if Moses were replaced. He probably sounded like one of our modern-day political hatchet men as he pounded away at Moses' record. And it must have worked, too, because he ended up with a band of 250 supporters.

Korah must have felt emboldened as leader after leader pledged support to his cause. In fact, many scholars believe he even set up a sort of campaign headquarters, a cluster of tents that could well have been designed to compete with the tabernacle that Moses had built (Num. 16:23–26).

But Korah was forgetting that Moses wasn't in his position of leadership because he wanted to be. He was in that position because God put him there! Indeed, Moses had tried everything he could think of to avoid leading the people, but God wouldn't take no for an answer. So Korah wasn't attacking Moses as much as he was attacking God. And in case you haven't noticed, people who attack God always end up regretting it.

In this particular case, Moses, feeling the heat, approached God and said, in essence, "What do You want me to do? If You want me to resign, that's fine. If You'd prefer to have Korah lead Your people, that's okay with me. I'll just step aside."

But God had other ideas.

First, He caused the earth to split open so that it swallowed Korah, his two sidekicks, and their families. They were standing there smirking one minute, and the next they were falling deep into the hot belly of the earth. (I guess you could say they took the express elevator to hell.) And when they were gone, the earth rumbled a second time and came back together (Num. 16:33).

Oh, but God wasn't finished.

Next he turned his sights on the 250 leaders who had joined

Korah's rebellion. Verse 35 says that "fire blazed forth from the LORD" and burned them up. We don't know if it was a blowtorch-like stream of fire coming down from heaven or if it was something more on the order of spontaneous combustion. But it got the job done. In what must have been a matter of minutes, Korah's rebellion was finished.

Or was it?

In a truly stunning twist, verse 41 says, "But the very next morning the whole community began muttering again against Moses and Aaron, saying, 'You two have killed the LORD's people!'"

What were they thinking?

First, the manner in which Korah and his cohorts died made it obvious that a power far greater than Moses was involved. And second, since the people were killed for speaking against Moses, why in the world would they want to start criticizing Moses all over again the very next day? I mean, really. Were those people taking stupid pills, or what?

So, once again, God set about the business of cleaning house. This time He sent a plague. What kind, we don't know. But it must have been a bad one because we're told that before Aaron could intercede on the people's behalf and persuade God to stop it, 14,700 people were dead.

So now, let's do the math.

Korah, his buddies, and their families were killed in the earthquake; 250 of his followers were killed in the fire; and 14,700 complainers were killed by the plague. That makes close to 15,000 deaths, and every one of them was unnecessary.

You see, that's the point.

The people were already on a hard road. Every day was already a challenge. But suddenly, as a result of pure disobedience, they complicated their lives exponentially. Imagine the pall of grief that must have hung over the entire camp! Think of all the graves that had to be dug. Picture the plague-poisoned bodies piled up and the stench of death that must have blown throughout the entire camp. Think of all the husbands and wives who were suddenly widowed and all the children who were orphaned. Solomon could have been offering a commentary on this very story when he said, "They must eat the bitter fruit of living their own way. They must experience the full terror of the path they have chosen" (Prov. 1:31).

But it could have been different.

If only the people had obeyed. If only they had respected God's wishes and gotten with the program, they could have avoided all of those horrors. Their journey still wouldn't have been easy, but it would have been *easier*. And when you're on a hard road, you need all the *easier* you can get!

Always remember, while junk will always accumulate in your life, you have control over the rate of accumulation. By committing to strict obedience you can avoid a lot of unnecessary burdens.

As I close this chapter, let me encourage you to take a hard look at your lifestyle. Are there some attitudes or behavior patterns in your life that are only making your hard road harder? Is it possible that a few simple adjustments could go a long way toward straightening your road and lightening your load? Maybe only one key lifestyle change is all it would take to make a huge difference. If so, I challenge you to make it. As Hebrews 12:1 says, "Let us strip off every weight that slows us down, especially the sin that so easily hinders our progress."

Two people can accomplish more than twice as much as one; they get a better return for their labor. If one person falls, the other can reach out and help. But people who are alone when they fall are in real trouble. And on a cold night, two under the same blanket can gain warmth from each other. But how can one be warm alone? A person standing alone can be attacked and defeated, but two can stand back-to-back and conquer.

—ECCLESIASTES 4:9–12

Travel with a Friend

What good fellowship we enjoyed
as we walked together to the house of God.

—PSALM 55:14

It happened on Memorial Day, 1995.

Christopher Reeve, famous for playing Superman in the movies, was competing in a riding competition in Culpeper, Virginia. After a smooth warm-up on his trusted horse, Buck, he left the starting box and headed for the first jump.

He executed it flawlessly.

The second jump was also perfect.

It was the third one that landed him on a road he never wanted to travel.

For some reason, Buck slammed on the breaks just as he got to the fence. There'd been no warning, nothing in the animal's behavior that suggested something was wrong. Later, some speculated that a rabbit had run across his path. Others wondered if there might have been an unexpected sound or a shadow. Either way, Buck came to a skidding halt, a "dirty stop" as it's known in the sport, because the rider has no chance to prepare.

Christopher Reeve went flying off the horse, headfirst. His hands were entangled in the reins, causing him to jerk the bridle and bit right off Buck's face. It also meant that he couldn't get his hands free to break his fall. He landed on his head on the other side of the fence and suffered what's called a "hangman's injury." The term comes from the days when men were hanged for their crimes. It's what happens when the trapdoor opens and the rope snaps tight. The result is a severe spinal cord injury and instant paralysis.

Christopher Reeve's body was badly damaged, but thanks to the helmet he was wearing, his mind wasn't. For that reason, he was able to be very productive after the injury. From his wheelchair, he wrote books, acted, directed, gave speeches, and worked tirelessly to promote various social causes, including spinal cord injury research. Some say his postinjury accomplishments were more notable than his preinjury accomplishments.

In Reeve's book, *Still Me*, which was written three years after the accident, you'll find an interesting photograph. He's reclining on a physical therapy table with his breathing tube attached. He appears to be propped up a little, and his lovely wife, Dana, is at his side. Her arm is draped across his chest, and her smiling face is nuzzled against his shoulder. It's the caption that I found so touching. Referring to his wife, he says: *"My 'medication'—better than any drug they ever gave me."*

They say a picture is worth a thousand words, and it must be true because, when I saw that photograph, I knew it perfectly communicated the idea I wanted to get across in this chapter. It's simply this: The hard roads of life are best traveled with a friend. Even though God will be walking with you every step of the way, there's a benefit to human companionship that cannot be denied.

Much of my time over the last thirty years has been spent in the company of hard-road travelers. I've advised them, cried with them, prayed with them, and buried their loved ones. But most of all, I've listened to them. And what I've learned from their stories is the value and the power of friendship. Many, like Christopher Reeve, point to their spouses. Others point to a pastor or doctor or neighbor. But they *all* point to someone and acknowledge that that person is "better than any drug."

Sadly, there's a tendency in our self-obsessed culture to downplay the importance of friendship when it comes to facing life's challenges. On a recent visit to our local Borders bookstore, I found the following titles sitting conspicuously on the shelves:

- *Self-Empowerment*
- *Coach Yourself to Success*
- *You Can Heal Your Life*
- *What You Feel You Can Heal*
- *You Can Make It Happen*
- *Setting Yourself Free*
- *Help Yourself*
- *Superself*
- *Healing Yourself with Self-Hypnosis*

As their titles suggest, the common theme of these books is that you have what it takes within yourself to make it through any problem. But, again, real life doesn't bear that out. I've yet to find a single hard-road survivor who claims to have made it alone. Even if at first he thought he could, he quickly discovered that what Solomon said is true: "Two are better than one" (Eccl. 4:9 NIV).

Of course, two have *always* been better than one.

When God first made man, He said that it wasn't good for him to be alone. And if it wasn't good for him to be alone in the safe haven of the Garden of Eden, how much more dangerous is it for him to be alone in a fallen world where the roads are hard and evil lurks in every shadow? First Peter 5:8 says that Satan "prowls around like a roaring lion, looking for some victim to devour." Notice, that's *victim*, singular. He picks people off one at a time. He targets the person traveling alone. This is why Jesus sent His evangelists out in pairs (Luke 10:1).

If the path of your life has recently veered off into the wilderness, don't even think about trying to go it alone. You may think of yourself as a strong person—and you may well be—but the wilderness has a way of chewing up even the strongest people and spitting them out.

Find a Friend

Let me encourage you to find yourself a traveling companion—a friend who will walk with you, support you, and encourage you every step of the way.

Just be very careful whom you choose!

Some of your current friends and family members will not be qualified to fulfill this crucial role. They may think they are and they may mean well, but they may lack the faith, patience, and experience necessary to offer the kind of assistance you'll need. Establishing a relationship with the wrong person could, in fact, make your journey even harder.

I believe the model for the kind of person you need by your side is seen in Moses. If the Israelites had a friend, he was it. Granted, they didn't always view him as a friend. There were times when they wanted to lynch him. But I don't know of anyone who thinks that ragtag bunch of former slaves would have made it through the wilderness without him. Clearly, he made a huge difference.

Let me point out four qualities that make a person a perfect hard-road companion.

The first would be *wilderness experience*. Moses was highly qualified to lead the Israelites through a wilderness because he'd been living in one for years. After growing up in Pharaoh's household, he fled to Midian after killing a man in a fit of rage. There he met and married a girl and began tending her father's sheep. Exodus 3:1 says he was doing just that, deep in the wilderness near Sinai, when he saw the burning bush and heard the voice of God calling him to return to Egypt and lead His people. He'd had no idea those years of wilderness living were preparing him for his life's calling.

A few years ago, Poinciana Christian Church went through a very difficult building program. A facility that should have been built in twelve months took thirty-three months to complete—and not for a lack of funds. It seemed that every week brought a new and unexpected problem. County officials and subcontractors shook their heads in amazement. One fellow told me that he never believed in curses till he started working on our project. It was a hard road, to say the least, easily the darkest and most difficult period of my life in the ministry.

About the time our project started to get complicated, I discovered that another church nearby had had a similar experience. Immediately I called the pastor and asked if we could meet. Over lunch we swapped stories, and I was stunned to realize how closely my experience was mirroring his. I knew when we parted that day that I'd found a traveling companion. Over the next several months, we talked numerous times. One day I called him and didn't even say hello. As soon as he answered, I said, "Give me one reason why I shouldn't give up." He did better than that. He gave me a half dozen. I know I wouldn't have made it without him.

And now, guess what has happened.

Two days ago I received a phone call from a pastor not far away. He said, "I've heard about the struggles you had with your building program. Right now we're having a terrible time with ours. I was wondering if you could come and speak to our church. We're all discouraged over here, and we need someone to give us some hope."

I was honored to say yes to his request. In fact, I spent a half hour encouraging him on the phone. Just before we hung up, he said, "Wow, this has been great. I should have called you months ago." I knew just how he felt. When you're stuck in a wilderness, it's wonderful to meet up with someone who has wilderness experience.

Second, the perfect hard-road companion will have *an intimate connection with God*. Perhaps the most striking thing about Moses was his relationship with God. It got off to a rough start as he stood in the glow of the burning bush and argued with God for all he was worth (Ex. 3:11–13). But once it got rolling, it was a thing to behold. Exodus 33:11 says, "Inside the Tent of Meeting, the LORD would speak to Moses face to face, as a man speaks to his friend."

It's a good thing Moses was so well connected with God, because there were times when the people weren't connected with Him at all. There were times when God was so fed up with them that He was ready to wipe them out and start over. And He would have if Moses hadn't interceded on their behalf (Ex. 32:9–13).

Which brings up an important point:

As a hard-road traveler, there will be times when you, too, will feel disconnected from God. Not that you'll rebel as the Israelites did, but you'll have hard days—days when you're so frustrated or discouraged or angry that you won't be able to pray. In fact, you may not even *want* to. Or even if you do, the words just may not come.

Not long ago, a woman in our church who is on a very hard road told me that even though she's been a Christian for more than twenty years and loves the Lord with all her heart, there are days when God seems like a complete stranger to her. If you haven't had that feeling yet, you will.

And that's when your traveling companion will be a tremendous help. He (or she) will be your bridge to God. Not by scolding or lecturing, but simply by loving you unconditionally. By allowing you to yell and scream if you need to. By allowing you to express yourself without any fear of being judged. And by searching the Scriptures and praying with you.

It would be ideal if your traveling companion happened to be an older, more experienced Christian, though that certainly wouldn't be a prerequisite. It's just that wiser and more experienced Christians tend to naturally pull us up toward their level, which is important when our spirits are sagging to begin with. As a hard-road traveler, you're going to face plenty of challenges. You don't need the additional challenge of dragging along a weaker brother or sister.

Third, the perfect hard-road companion will have *a heart of compassion.* My favorite television show of all time is *The Andy Griffith Show.* In one unforgettable episode, Andy has to be out of town for the day and reluctantly leaves Barney in charge. When he returns, he finds Barney standing in front of the courthouse, grinning from ear to ear. The streets seem unusually quiet and Andy breathes a sigh of relief. Apparently, Barney has succeeded in keeping the peace in Mayberry.

But Andy is about to get a big surprise.

When they step inside the courthouse, he discovers that Barney has half the town locked up in jail. God-fearing, law-abiding citizens—including the mayor and Aunt Bee—have been arrested for everything from jaywalking to littering. Andy is horrified, of course, not to mention the good citizens themselves. But Barney is beaming with pride. He sees no problem. As far as he is concerned, justice was served in every single case.

We chuckle at such silliness, but isn't the world full of Barney Fifes? Isn't the world full of good people who mean well but are far too rigid? They know all the rules frontward and backward but don't have an ounce of understanding. On the other hand, the Andys of this world are far too few in number. They are the people who always seem to be cutting others some slack, giving them the benefit of the doubt, and offering whatever encouragement they can to help them on their way.

Obviously, if you're going to be traveling a hard road, you don't want Barney for a traveling companion. You don't want somebody who's going to watch you like a hawk and blow the whistle every time you say or do something wrong. Instead, you want Andy. You want somebody who will show you some compassion.

My old dog-eared Webster's dictionary defines *compassion* as "actively sympathetic concern for the suffering of another." The word *actively* is the key. You'd have to have a heart of stone not to feel "sympathetic concern" for suffering people. But feeling it and demonstrating it are two different things. True compassion is always active.

I love the story about the four-year-old boy who saw his next-door neighbor, an elderly gentleman, sitting on his porch, weeping after his wife's funeral. Without saying a word, he walked over, climbed up on the old man's lap, and just sat there. Later, his mother, who'd been watching out the window, asked him what he said to the old man. The little boy answered, "Nothing; I just helped him cry."

Romans 12:15 says, "When others are happy, be happy with them. If they are sad, share their sorrow."

That's compassion.

Finally, the perfect hard-road companion will be *loyal*. Hard roads are seldom short roads. In fact, many hard roads have no end this side of heaven. Think again about Christopher Reeve. He talked optimistically about being able to walk again, but it didn't happen. He, like countless other people, had to live with the results of his injury the rest of his life.

I've noticed over the years that when a person first lands on a hard road, there's an outpouring of love and support. If you receive a shocking diagnosis, lose your job, or experience a death in the family, people will almost overwhelm you with encouragement. But as time passes, interest in your situation will begin to wane. It's not that people stop caring. It's simply that life goes on. Have you noticed how a front-page news story will slowly work its way toward the back of the paper and eventually disappear altogether? It has nothing to do with the importance of the story. It has to do with the fact that new things are happening every day that need to be reported, and people want to know about those new things. This is one of the beautiful things about walking with a loyal and trusted friend on your hard road. To that person, you're always front-page news.

Again, here are the qualities you should look for in a traveling companion:

- Wilderness experience
- An intimate connection with God
- Compassion
- Loyalty

Obviously, any person who possesses these qualities will be a treasure. In fact, you may be wondering if such people even exist anymore. I can tell you that they do, and they are most commonly found in churches. The church has taken a lot of heat over the years, and much of it has been deserved. But I've still never found another organization or institution that offers more help and encouragement to hard-road travelers.

Several years ago, an elderly lady in our church died a slow death from cancer. People in general were very good to her, but one young man in particular was amazing. Every day for almost a year, he stopped to visit her on his way home from work. Sometimes he stayed five minutes and sometimes he stayed an hour. But he always stopped, he always had a word of encouragement for her, and he always prayed with her before he left. On several occasions she told me that she didn't know what she would do without him. And here's the critical point: Their only connection was our church. They weren't related. They weren't neighbors. They hadn't been lifelong friends. They only found each other because one day they wound up sitting side by side in the same worship service.

As a pastor, I can tell you that suffering and adversity often drive people to church. Many of the people I meet for the first time are hurting in some way and are desperately looking for God. They often find Him, but not always in the form they expect. The lady I just mentioned found Him in the heart of a guy wearing blue jeans and a polo shirt. He sat down beside her, stuck out his hand, and said, "Hi, my name is Michael. What's yours?"

Honestly, I love that about God.

I love the fact that He does so much of his work through ordinary people. There's something kind of mind-boggling about the almighty God of the universe using stuttering tongues and clumsy hands to bring healing and hope to those in need. A miracle would be so much quicker and easier, not to mention more impressive.

But God loves to partner with His children, and a great deal of that partnering happens in church.

If it's been a while since you were part of a church family, maybe now would be a good time to reestablish that part of your life.

Value Your Friend

Because Poinciana Christian Church is so close to Disney World, a number of our members are employed there. Before they are allowed to work a single day, they go through something called "Traditions," where they are drilled on the finer points of professional etiquette. They are taught to smile and to be helpful and courteous at all times. They are trained to handle even the most difficult situations (and the most difficult people) with grace and humility. And if you've ever been to the parks, you know it works. You'd be hard-pressed to find a friendlier place on the planet.

But you should hear some of the stories my Disney friends tell me.

They're often treated rudely by guests. They're yelled at and screamed at for no reason. And they're blamed for things they have no control over. One friend told me about the time a guest went on a tirade because she and her family had been in Orlando for three days and it had rained every day—as if my friend had any control over the weather! But through it all, those cast members manage to keep right on smiling.

Well, most of the time.

At least on the outside.

The point is that sometimes the best people receive the worst treatment. One of the first things you'll notice about the wilderness journey of the Israelites is that they didn't value Moses the way they should have. They blamed him for every problem and grumbled endlessly about his leadership without ever stopping to realize that they wouldn't have been in the wilderness in the first place if they'd simply followed his instructions and entered the Promised Land when they had the opportunity.

Let me encourage you to be careful how you treat the friend who's walking with you on your hard road. There will be days when you'll be more cranky and critical than usual. Little things that ordinarily wouldn't bother you will tick you off big-time. Of course, such responses to discomfort are normal, but they can also be your undoing if they drive away all the people who really care about you. Sure, chances are good that your traveling companion will understand and tolerate a certain amount of expressed frustration. Everybody knows it goes with the territory. But prolonged periods of disagreeable conduct will wear down even your most faithful friend.

Remember that the person who's walking with you obviously loves you and is no doubt making some real sacrifices to help you along the way. Always do your best to treat him or her accordingly.

My first book, *The Samson Syndrome* (Nelson, 2003), focused on a man who is, perhaps, the greatest enigma of Scripture. Gifted as few men have ever been, Samson had the opportunity to become the greatest hero in the Bible, other than Jesus. But it never happened. His life deteriorated into a tawdry soap opera as he fell prey to one temptation after another. What's striking is that Samson, by choice, traveled alone. We never see him with a sidekick, a buddy, or a mentor. Unlike Moses, who had Aaron; or Joshua, who had Caleb; or David, who had Jonathan; or Paul, who had Barnabas and Silas . . . Samson had nobody. He wandered the hard roads of life all by himself and paid a terrible price. Even his legendary physical strength wasn't enough to help him meet and overcome the challenges he faced.

You may be gifted too. You may be stronger than anyone you know.

But don't be fooled. Your hard road will get you if you try to go it alone.

Travel with a friend.

Tell the people to purify themselves, for tomorrow they will have meat to eat. Tell them, "The LORD has heard your whining and complaints: 'If only we had meat to eat! Surely we were better off in Egypt!' Now the LORD will give you meat, and you will have to eat it. And it won't be for just a day or two, or for five or ten or even twenty. You will eat it for a whole month until you gag and are sick of it. For you have rejected the LORD, who is here among you, and you have complained to him, 'Why did we ever leave Egypt?'"

—NUMBERS 11:18–20

Stay Positive

When the LORD heard your complaining,
he became very angry.

—DEUTERONOMY 1:34

There will be many tough battles you'll have to fight as you travel your hard road, but none will be tougher than the battle to stay positive. You may be a happy, upbeat person by nature, but when the circumstances of your life take a nasty turn and you suddenly realize you're looking at a long, painful journey, you will not be able to stop the negative thoughts from rushing into your mind. It will seem as if somebody turned on a spigot inside your head. They will flood every nook and cranny of your brain.

Countless books and articles have been written about the benefits of a positive attitude. In this chapter, I don't intend to plow that ground again. Instead, I want to focus on what I believe is by far the most important issue for hard-road travelers to consider when it comes to the subject of one's attitude. It's simply that your attitude will profoundly affect your relationship with God.

We can see it with the Israelites. They were God's chosen people and He loved them deeply, but their constant whining and complaining triggered His wrath like nothing else they ever did. Psalm 78 pictures this very vividly. After talking about all the wonderful things God did for them—everything from parting the waters of the Red Sea and delivering them from the Egyptians, to providing fresh water for them in the wilderness—it says:

> Yet they kept on with their sin, rebelling against the Most High in the desert. They willfully tested God in their hearts, demanding the foods they craved. They even spoke against God himself, saying, "God can't give us food in the desert. Yes, he can strike a rock so water gushes out, but he can't give his people bread and meat." When the LORD heard them, he was angry. The fire of his wrath burned against Jacob. Yes, his anger rose against Israel, for they did not believe God or trust him to care for them. (vv. 17–22)

Friend, mark it down. Nothing will drive a wedge between you and God, nothing will stem the flow of His blessings into your life, like a complaining spirit. The Bible makes it clear that certain things really tick God off, and a whiny mouth is at the top of the list. It ignites His anger like a lit match falling into a pool of gasoline. And why shouldn't it? After all He's done for us, surely He has the right to expect us to show a little gratitude! As a parent, doesn't it infuriate you when you knock yourself out to meet every need your children have, only to hear them grousing about all the things they *don't* have?

But still, we are human, and it's hard to be positive when life dumps us in the middle of a wilderness. Right now, you may be agreeing intellectually with everything I'm saying, yet still feel like you want to spit on the carpet and kick the dog. For that reason, I want to spend the rest of this chapter exploring some simple ideas that I believe will help you stay positive (or regain your positive attitude) and maintain a healthy relationship with the One whose support you simply must have if you hope to make it through your ordeal.

Remember: Things Could Always Be Worse

In our church there is an elderly lady who's been a shut-in for the last couple of years. She's had her knees replaced, major cancer surgery, and a couple of eye surgeries, along with a host of smaller procedures. But I love to go see her because she's always so upbeat. No matter how bad she's feeling, she always puts on a happy face and tells me how blessed she is. In fact, she has a little rhyme that she never fails to quote when I ask how she's doing. She says:

> From the time you're born till you ride in a hearse,
> Things are never so bad that they couldn't be worse.

How true.

One of the creepiest stories in the Bible focuses on the occasion when God taught this truth to His people. It was during the wilderness period, and the people were on the move. They were dragging all their stuff across an ugly landscape that never seemed to change. The weather was scorching, their gear was getting heavier with every step, and their muscles ached as never before. What's worse, there didn't seem to be any end in sight. So, right on cue, they began bellyaching to God and Moses: "Why have you brought us out of Egypt to die here in the wilderness? . . . There is nothing to eat here and nothing to drink. And we hate this wretched manna!" (Num. 21:5).

I cringe every time I read those words.

Everybody knows there are just some things you don't do. You don't spit into the wind. You don't tell an airport security inspector that you're going to Afghanistan to visit your uncle Osama. You don't pull up behind a motorcycle gang on the freeway and lay on your horn. And above all, you don't tell God that you "hate" His "wretched" blessings. If you do, you're going to be sorry. Really sorry.

Numbers 21:6 says, "So the LORD sent poisonous snakes among them, and many of them were bitten and died."

Let me just say right here that I hate snakes. I don't mean I dislike them. I don't mean I would prefer not to be around them. I mean, I *hate* them. To me, the only good snake is a dead snake, and anybody who feels otherwise, in my mind, needs prayer and counseling. I despise snakes. Especially when they are where they don't belong.

Like in a house.

A few years ago I led a jazz quartet and we were rehearsing at the drummer's house. We were plowing through one of our up-tempo arrangements when his wife walked into the room looking as if she'd just seen a ghost. We stopped the music and waited for her to say something, but she was speechless. Her husband said, "What's wrong, honey?" She still didn't say anything, but in zombielike fashion, motioned for us to follow. We put down our instruments and followed her through the house and into the master bedroom, finally stopping in the doorway of the master bath.

What I saw almost gave me a heart attack.

There, lying on the vanity counter, was a three-foot-long snake. I don't know what kind it was. As far as I was concerned, it was a king cobra. Its body was woven in and around some cologne bottles and draped over one of the faucet handles. How it got there, we don't know to this day.

The piano player looked at me and said, "What are we going to do?"

I shot back, "We? What do you mean, 'we'?" Then I pointed to the drummer and said, "It's *his* house. That makes it *his* snake." And I was gone.

Every time I read this story about God's punishment of His people, I remember that incident and get the willies. Having a snake in the house is just over-the-top creepy. So you can imagine how terrifying it must have been for the Israelites to have them in their drawers, cupboards, beds, and even in their food supplies. And poisonous snakes, to boot! Everywhere they turned they found beady eyes, darting tongues, and flashing fangs.

But you see what God was doing, don't you? He wasn't being mean. He was teaching His children a lesson they desperately needed to learn. He was showing them how much worse their circumstances could be. Remember, they weren't complaining because they were starving. They had plenty to eat. They were complaining because their dinner menu didn't include prime rib and yeast rolls! So God said, "You think that's a problem? Let Me show you what a *real* problem is!" And suddenly, poisonous snakes were slithering through every crack and crevice in their homes.

And it worked!

Suddenly, with shrieks ringing throughout the camp and corpses starting to pile up, the people cried out to Moses, "We have sinned by speaking against the LORD and against you. Pray that the LORD will take away the snakes" (21:7). Oh, how they wanted things to go back to the way they were! Suddenly their former circumstances didn't seem so bad. Of course, God did take away the snakes. And don't you know their manna never tasted so good?

You'll find it easier to remain positive if you remember that even though your situation may be bad, it really could be worse.

Remember: Things Could Be Better
Than You Think They Are

In November 2002, Marilyn and I moved into our current home. It backs up to a man-made pond that's about four hundred feet long and a hundred feet wide. It winds through our neighborhood in an S shape, giving about a dozen homeowners the privilege of saying they own waterfront property. It's not a very majestic body of water, I'll admit. But it sure is pretty, especially when the radiant colors of a Florida sunset are reflecting off its ripples. We have affectionately dubbed it "Lake Atteberry."

As we were unpacking on the day we moved in, I said to Marilyn, "I wonder if there are any fish in there." She said, "Why don't you grab your rod and go find out?" And I'll admit I was tempted. But then a steady stream of negative thoughts started flowing into my mind. First, I hadn't seen any of the other homeowners fishing. Second, I hadn't seen any of the ripples or swirls that frolicking fish often make. And third, I couldn't imagine the developer of the subdivision wanting to spend the money it would take to stock all the ponds in the neighborhood. "No," I said, "I'm sure I'd be wasting my time if I went out there. And the neighbors would probably laugh at me. They'd say, 'Look at that fool out there fishing in a pond that doesn't have any fish in it!'"

That was nineteen months ago.

For more than a year and a half, I looked longingly at Lake Atteberry, trying to convince myself to toss in a little yellow Rooster Tail and just see if anything would hit it. But every single time, those same negative thoughts started bubbling up and caused me to put the idea out of my head. Oh yes, I saw some circles in the water and heard a few splashes now and then. But I told myself they were being made by bugs or frogs or tadpoles or turtles. Anything but fish.

And then, about two weeks ago, everything changed.

I was working in the garage and came face-to-face with my ultralight spinning rod. It was standing up in the corner and still had a little white Shyster attached to the swivel. Suddenly, my fisherman's heart leaped in my chest and I felt an overwhelming urge to pick it up, walk out the back door, and make a few casts. At almost the same instant, a tiny voice from somewhere inside me said, *But the neighbors will think you're nuts!* And then another voice answered, *So what? Half the people who know you think you're nuts. What difference will a few more make?* And just that quickly, I was marching toward Lake Atteberry with rod in hand. I had broken through a wall. I was a man on a mission. It was all I could do to keep from breaking into a trot.

I'll admit that when I got to the water's edge, I looked around to see if any of the neighbors might be watching. I didn't see anyone, so I pressed the lever on my little Zebco, drew the rod back past my ear, and let 'er fly. The little lure flew forward in a lazy arc and plopped in the water about fifteen feet in front of me. Not exactly reminiscent of Bill Dance, but hey, I hadn't thrown a cast in a couple of years. Quickly, I reeled it in and threw another one. This time the lure went perhaps five feet farther and must have landed right on top of a fish's head.

Wham!

I had barely started cranking when something hit the lure hard. Of course, on an ultralight every fish feels like Moby Dick, but this guy was obviously no guppy. And boy, did he have a mean streak! He ripped and darted under the water while I held my breath and tried not to lose him. A few seconds later, I pulled out a nice big bluegill that was about the size of my hand. (Again, I looked around to see if any neighbors were watching. Only this time, I was hoping they were!)

My heart was racing.

I was ecstatic!

But I didn't know whether to jump for joy or kick myself.

For a year and a half I'd had a nice little fishing hole just seventy-five feet out my back door, but not once had I even attempted to catch a fish. I hate to think how many hours of relaxation and enjoyment were forever lost to me during that time simply because I allowed a series of negative thoughts to form a conga line in my brain.

And I must tell you, I am not a pessimist! Ask anybody who knows me. I am normally a very optimistic, upbeat person. Yet I go through those periods when my negativity gene flares up and I think myself into an emotional tailspin. I convince myself of things that simply are not true. I blow problems out of proportion. I assume the worst.

However, I don't beat myself up over it, because I know I'm in good company. For example, Elijah did the same thing. When he heard that Jezebel wanted him dead, his negativity gene flared up and he thought himself into a deep depression. And talk about exaggerating his circumstances! He convinced himself that he was the only person left in Israel who was faithful to the Lord, when in fact there were seven thousand others who hadn't bowed their knees to Baal (1 Kings 19:14–18)!

Be honest now. Haven't you done this sort of thing before? Haven't there been times when you blew your problems out of proportion or convinced yourself that things were worse than they really were?

Deny it if it makes you feel better, but I've never met a person who didn't have the ability to turn a molehill into Mount Everest. It's just part of being human. And it means that maybe—just maybe—your current circumstances might not be as bad as they seem at the moment. Perhaps your negativity gene is on its high horse and kicking up a fuss in your brain. Or maybe there are certain positive aspects of your circumstances you've overlooked or that haven't made themselves evident yet. Either way, it's entirely possible that things could be better than you think they are.

Remember: Things Are in Good Hands

If you sat down in a restaurant and learned that Emeril Lagasse was in the kitchen and would be preparing your meal, would you be worried about whether the food would be fit to eat?

If you were informed by your contractor that Bob Vila would be overseeing your kitchen remodeling project, would you be worried about whether the work was going to be done right?

If you took your son to Little League sign-ups and learned that Tony LaRussa was going to be coaching his team, would you be worried about whether he would learn the fundamentals of baseball?

If you walked into your church next Sunday morning and learned that Max Lucado was going to be preaching, would you be worried about whether the sermon would be worth listening to?

Isn't it true that sometimes there's just nothing to worry about because things are in good hands? And if that's true of cooking and carpentry and baseball and preaching, isn't it even more true of the circumstances of our lives, considering they are in God's hands? After all, He created life. More to the point, He created you! Doesn't that qualify Him as an expert?

Think about it.

We consider Emeril an expert, but he didn't invent cooking.

We consider Bob Vila an expert, but he didn't invent carpentry.

We consider Tony LaRussa an expert, but he didn't invent baseball.

And we consider Max Lucado an expert, but he didn't invent preaching.

How much more of an expert does that make God, considering He *is* the Designer and Creator of everything? Psalm 24:1–2 says, "The earth is the LORD's, and everything in it. The world and all its people belong to him. For he laid the earth's foundation on the seas and built it on the ocean depths."

That's a pretty impressive résumé, isn't it?

Do you know anybody who has one better?

Friend, believe it. Things are in good hands. The sovereign Lord and Creator of the universe knows what's going on in your life and is monitoring the situation moment by moment. Psalm 121:8 says, "The LORD keeps watch over you as you come and go, both now and forever."

And not only does He watch over you and monitor your circumstances; if you're a Christian, He carefully maneuvers them to your ultimate advantage. Romans 8:28 says, "God causes everything to work together for the good of those who love God and are called according to his purpose for them."

The question is, do you believe these promises are true? If you're not sure, let me call a few witnesses to testify on God's behalf.

First, say hello to Joseph:

I was just seventeen when my ten older brothers kidnapped me and sold me into slavery. Honestly, I thought my life was over. I figured I'd live out my days busting rocks and feeling the crack of a whip across my back. I thought I'd never see another happy day. But just thirteen years later I found myself sitting in a palace, calling the shots for the most powerful nation on earth. It was simply amazing how God worked every situation to my advantage. Sometimes things moved slowly. At times I had to be very patient. But over time, God brought me to a place I could never have reached on my own. As I look back, it's clear that what my brothers meant for evil, God meant for good. (See Genesis 37–50.)

Next I'd like you to hear what a poor, nameless widow has to say:

Have you ever been hungry? I'm not talking about those times when your stomach rumbles because you're running late for dinner. I'm referring to the kind of body-numbing weakness that builds up in you over a period of weeks because you're eating less and less every day. That's the situation my son and I were in. In fact, we came to the place where we had enough flour and oil to cook one more meal. We knew it would be our last because the famine we were enduring showed no signs of letting up. So we put our affairs in order and said good-bye to a few close friends. For my son's sake, I tried to act cheerful. I talked a lot about going to be with the Lord and how much better off we would be. But truth be told, my heart was breaking. Several times I had to turn away so he wouldn't see me brush a tear from my cheek.

It was while I was out picking up a few sticks for the fire that a stranger approached and asked me for something to eat. It was all I could do to keep from laughing in his face. "Mister, you're barking up the wrong tree," I said bitterly. But the smile—or was it a smirk?—never left his face. Either this guy was a jerk, or he knew something I didn't.

The latter turned out to be the case.

His name was Elijah, and he was a prophet that God sent to save me and my son. I can't explain how it worked. In fact, I don't even care. All I know is, after he arrived, our supplies of flour and oil never diminished. No matter how much we used, there was always enough left in the containers for one more meal. (See 1 Kings 17:8–16.)

And finally, I'd like to ask Daniel to say a few words:

How many good ways are there to die? Not many, I suppose. I'd always hoped I would die in my sleep. You know, just go to bed some evening and wake up in heaven. So you can imagine how I felt when

I was sentenced to death in a lions' den. The very idea of being ripped limb from limb by those razor-sharp teeth caused me to break out in a cold sweat. And, to be honest, I could have avoided it. All I had to do was stop praying to God and bow down to King Darius. But it wasn't in me to do that. God had been faithful to me for so long that I couldn't bring myself to turn against Him just because I was being threatened.

So into the lions' den I went.

And, boy, was it creepy.

The stench of raw meat hung in the air, and there were bloodstains on the floor of the cave. It was obvious that a lot of people had died in that room! But the next morning I walked out of that den in perfect health. You see, God didn't let me go in there alone. He sent an angel in with me to shut the lions' mouths. I'm telling you, they were as meek as pussycats all night long! If I'd only had a ball of yarn or a rubber mouse, we could have had such fun together! (See Daniel 6.)

Joseph, the widow of Zarephath, and Daniel are only three of the countless hard-road travelers who would gladly attest to God's faithfulness in managing the circumstances of our lives. They would rise as a gigantic choir from the pages of history and say with one voice, "Don't worry. Things are in good hands!"

Do you believe it?

Ultimately, that is the all-important question.

If you do believe it, you will always have a reason to smile. Even on your darkest days, you can keep moving forward with a sense of anticipation. You can rest assured that God is wide awake and watching over you—and ready to intervene if necessary.

Before I close this chapter, I want to tell you about a group of hard-road travelers who made up their minds to stay positive and are making a real impact on their world as a result. They are the members of a Miami-area softball team called the One-Arm Bandits. The name seems a little odd until you realize that twelve of the fifteen players on the team have only one arm. Some of them lost their arms in horrific accidents while others were born without an arm. But they still play, and quite well. They compete in a C-level fast-pitch league and also visit schools and hospitals, telling their stories and encouraging other handicapped people to stay positive.

Can you imagine not being able to hold a knife and fork to cut a steak, but telling yourself you can play fast-pitch softball against guys with no handicaps at all? That's what I call positive! And a lot of those guys are excelling in many other areas of their lives, too. You see, that's the thing about positive people. You just can't keep them down.

So no matter how tough things get, remember:

Things could always be worse.

Things could be better than you think they are.

And things are in good hands.

Because the men who explored the land were there for forty days, you must wander in the wilderness for forty years—a year for each day, suffering the consequences of your sins. You will discover what it is like to have me for an enemy." I, the LORD, have spoken! I will do these things to every member of the community who has conspired against me. They will all die here in this wilderness!

—NUMBERS 14:34–35

Step over the Dead
and Keep Going

Don't get discouraged and give up, for we will reap
a harvest of blessing at the appropriate time.
—GALATIANS 6:9

Think back to your nineteenth-century American history. Does the name James Marshall ring a bell?

I'd be surprised if it did. He's been all but forgotten, even though he is credited with making the single most important discovery in this country before 1900.

It was on January 24, 1847, that Mr. Marshall and about twenty other men were building a sawmill near what is now San Francisco. Their work was almost done when he looked down and saw something shiny in the dirt. He knelt to have a look at the object and saw another nearby. And then another. And another. They were little pea-sized nuggets, sparkling in the sunshine.

Sparkling like gold.

Purely by accident, James Marshall made the discovery that led to the great California Gold Rush. As news of his find reached the more heavily populated eastern states, "Go west, young man!" became a common catchphrase. And go west the young men did— in droves. During the next two years, ninety thousand people "rushed" to California with visions of wealth and privilege dancing in their heads.

Sadly, many thousands more died on the way.

The twenty-two-hundred-mile trip from Missouri to San Francisco was commonly made by wagon, at a speed of about two miles per hour, through some of the roughest and most dangerous terrain known to man. Also consider that many of those early pioneers were tenderfoots from civilized eastern cities, who had never experienced anything like the wild and woolly West. They had to face disease, Indians, stampeding cattle, blizzards, heat, lice, snakes, outlaws, and a lack of water. As a result, those westward trails became lined with freshly dug graves and makeshift cemeteries. It was said that those early prospectors passed a grave every day. And if they didn't pass one, they dug one.

Of all people, the Israelites could have related.

The wilderness road they traveled was also lined with graves and makeshift cemeteries. Because of their refusal to take the land of Canaan when He ordered them to, God decided that everyone twenty years of age and older (except for Caleb and Joshua) would die during the years of wandering (Num. 14:29–30). Granted, the deaths happened a few at a time, no doubt spread out over many years and many miles, but that didn't lessen the pain of the ordeal. Imagine the sadness and despair that must have hung heavy over those weary travelers as, day after day, more graves needed to be dug. Before they could finish grieving over one loved one, another would perish. By some estimates, as many as 1,200,000 Israelites would have died in the wilderness. That's about 30,000 a year; 2,500 a month; 625 a week; or 83 a day.

Just as surely as those Israelites died in the wilderness, many believers will die spiritually on the hard roads of our modern world. Yes, many will make it through and end up stronger and better people. That's the whole point of this book. But along every hard road you'll see the spiritual graves of those who fell along the way.

You'll see the grave of the man in extreme financial bondage who decided to compromise his integrity to make some fast money.

You'll see the grave of the unhappily married woman who decided to go home with a man who was not her husband.

You'll see the grave of the cancer patient who decided that God was the culprit rather than the answer.

Simply put, whenever despair swallows up the last vestige of hope, causing a hurting soul to surrender to the devil, a new spiritual grave will be dug.

Dealing with the Devil

The second Jesus' eyes fluttered open in the tomb, Satan knew his doom was sealed. He knew it was only a matter of time before Jesus returned and put him out of business once and for all, so he went to work with a ferocious sense of urgency. His goal for the last two thousand years has been twofold: to keep unbelievers right where they are and to destroy the faith of believers. Therefore, every grave you see along the hard road you happen to be traveling represents a victory for him. Every time a believer gives up the struggle, Satan laughs and thumbs his nose at God.

I have long believed that most Christians do not take the devil seriously enough. I mean, given his track record, you'd think we would batten down the hatches and set off all the alarms. But we don't. The following story illustrates the kind of apathy toward

Satan that I have been observing in my fellow believers for the last thirty years.

One cold December evening, Marilyn and I were chauffeuring a carload of ten-year-old girls to a church-sponsored Christmas party. They were crammed into the backseat, jabbering as only ten-year-old girls can, while we sat up front and listened. Their childish banter was amusing until one of the girls mentioned a movie she had watched the night before. My ears perked up. The film had recently been released on home video. I had seen the trailer on TV and knew it was a sleazy, R-rated cop caper. Immediately, two of the other girls confessed that they had seen it too. Then came the line that almost caused me to drive into the ditch. One of the girls mentioned how cute the leading man looked with no clothes on! This set off a cascade of giggles, which I vociferously interrupted with orders to change the subject.

I glanced at Marilyn and, even in the soft green glow of the dashboard lights, saw a stricken look on her face. We were shaken by that conversation because those little girls came from some of the finest families in our church. Why were their parents allowing them to watch movies containing gratuitous violence, profanity, and nudity? More to the point, why were their parents watching such movies themselves?

We have a freezer in our garage where we keep meat and other food items. One Saturday morning I unplugged it momentarily because I was doing an odd job nearby and needed to use the outlet. A few days later, I opened the freezer door to retrieve a carton of ice cream and was almost knocked to my knees by the stench. Everything was either melted or spoiled because I had forgotten to plug the freezer back in when I finished my work. It was all I could do to keep from gagging as I cleaned up the mess.

I have a question.

Why is it that people take great pains to dispose of their filthy, rotten kitchen garbage but then turn right around and allow their families to feed on filthy, rotten spiritual garbage? A parent would be charged with child abuse if he knowingly fed his children spoiled food, but he can allow them to watch a morally reprehensible DVD —and it's called entertainment!

I know some people will read this and call me an extremist. I've been having this debate with believers for years, and there are always those who accuse me of being too prudish and not living in the real world. My answer is that I believe I *am* living in the real world. The real world is a world where Satan is on the prowl, seeking someone to devour (1 Peter 5:8). He's trying to put every last one of us in a spiritual grave, and I have made up my mind that I will not make it easy for him. I refuse to throw open the front door of my home (or my heart) and let him come waltzing in like some long-lost cousin. Rather, I try my best to resist him, claiming God's promise that if I do, he will flee from me (James 4:7).

Briefly, I want to talk about the top four things you can do every day to confound and frustrate the devil's efforts to destroy you.

First, you can take control of your thought life. Remember Miss Cleo? Otherwise known as Youree Cleomili Harris, she was the so-called fortune-teller whose TV commercials saturated the airwaves a few years ago. Before she was shut down by the Federal Trade Commission, she made piles of money off people who were desperate to know where their lives were headed. What those poor victims didn't realize was that you don't need a fortune-teller to know where your life is headed. The Bible teaches that you're headed wherever your thoughts are focused. Look at this striking verse:

I opened my arms to my own people all day long, but they have rebelled. They follow their own evil paths and thoughts. (Isa. 65:2)

59

If there's one thing I've learned through my own Christian walk and thirty-plus years of ministry, it's that people follow their thoughts. I honestly can't name a single person I've ever met whose quality of life (for better or worse) wasn't a reflection of his or her thinking. People who think good, positive, wholesome, godly thoughts tend to be happier, stronger, and more able to deal with life's challenges than those who fill their minds with junk. No wonder Paul said, "Let God transform you into a new person by changing the way you think" (Rom. 12:2).

Right now, if your thought life is out of control, you need to take immediate action. I'm sure you wouldn't think of leaving all the doors and windows of your house open and unlocked twenty-four hours a day, so why would you do that with your mind? Why would you give Satan free access to the control center of your life? You know without a doubt that he will slide behind the wheel and steer you straight into trouble.

Let me encourage you to slam those doors and windows and lock them. Figure out where the negativity and filth are streaming into your mind and shut down those avenues. It won't be easy. In fact, it might require some radical changes in your lifestyle. You might have to break some habits or end some relationships, which will no doubt be unpleasant. But until you make those changes, Satan is going to have control over the direction of your life.

But don't stop there.

Take the next step and fill your mind with the Word of God. Ephesians 6:17 calls the Word of God "the sword of the Spirit." When I was a boy, my great-grandmother had a Civil War sword that had been passed down from one of her ancestors. I still remember what an imposing weapon it was. She wouldn't even let me touch it unless she was standing right there to supervise. Anybody swinging that thing would have made a terrifying opponent. And so it is that Satan hates to see a Christian swinging the sword of the Spirit. He knows very well that "the word of God cannot be chained" (2 Tim. 2:9). It is the greatest power in the universe.

If you're serious about resisting the devil, take control of your thought life.

Second, stay in fellowship with other people who are actively resisting the devil. Here we can draw a lesson from the redwood forests of California. Those giant trees can be as tall as three hundred feet, and fifty feet in diameter. You'd think the roots of such behemoths would reach deep into the earth, but they don't. Considering their height, redwoods actually have very shallow root systems. What, then, is the secret of their survival? How do they keep from toppling over when assailed by howling winds? Simple. Their roots, though shallow, are entangled with one another's. They are, in essence, locking arms and helping one another withstand nature's attacks.

I spoke about walking your hard road with a friend in Chapter 3, but here the idea is a little different. Those massive redwoods give us a beautiful picture of the church, that mighty forest of believers who have locked arms and are standing firm against Satan and his schemes. In my work as a pastor, I've seen how valuable the support of a loving church can be to any believer, but especially to one walking a hard road. I know countless people who would readily testify that they would never have made it through their wilderness without the love and encouragement of their church family.

Like Doris, for example.

She's a precious ninety-one-year-old lady in our church, and I visited her in the hospital today. She's been sick for a long, long time, and as I sat and chatted with her, I felt my eyes being drawn toward the foot of the bed. Every time she averted her eyes, I found myself sneaking a quick peek. Her legs were covered with a sheet, but still, I couldn't quit looking. You see, Doris's foot was amputated yesterday, and where her foot used to be, the sheet was lying flat against the mattress. It looked terribly odd and made me wonder how I would react if I were forced to give up one of my feet. Would Satan be able to access my heart through such a wound?

As usual, Doris's spirits were high. She told me she was thankful for two things. One, that God had allowed her to keep her foot for ninety-one years. (With a grin, she said, "My dancing days are over anyway, so what difference does it make?") And two, that she had a strong church family. She told me she would have given in to Satan's whispers long ago if not for the encouragement of her brothers and sisters. And as she spoke those words, one of her elderly church friends came tottering into the room with a big smile and a little bouquet of flowers. I watched as the two of them hugged and kissed. The joy I felt in my heart at that moment was indescribable.

Paul said, "Since we are all one body in Christ, we belong to each other, and each of us needs all the others" (Rom. 12:5). As a redwood tree needs its forest mates to help it withstand the attacks of nature, so we need our brothers and sisters in Christ to help us withstand what Doris called "Satan's whispers."

Third, if you're serious about resisting the devil, pray like crazy. James 5:16 says, "The earnest prayer of a righteous person has great power and wonderful results." Do you realize that the whole world is looking for wonderful results? It doesn't matter if you're running a business or raising children or living the Christian life, you want wonderful results. And bookstores are filled to overflowing with suggestions on how to get them. Yet the vast majority of those books neglect the element of prayer. In fact, many of the great success gurus of our time would judge prayer to be of little importance, if any.

Don't you believe it!

The Bible says that people don't have because they don't ask (James 4:2). It also says that we can be sure the Lord will give us what we ask for as long as what we ask for is in line with His will (1 John 5:14–15). Of course, there are other issues involved, such as timing (His isn't always what we prefer) and the free will God has granted to people. Even so, the Bible is clear in stating that we serve a prayer-answering God. That's why I agree with William Cowper, who said:

Satan trembles when he sees
The weakest saint upon his knees.

There's a wonderful story about two pastors' wives who were chatting as they mended their husbands' pants. One of them said, "My husband is so discouraged right now. There's trouble in the church, and it just seems the harder he works, the worse things get." The other woman said, "I've never seen my husband happier. It just seems God is blessing everything he does."

A thoughtful silence fell over the two women as they continued mending their husbands' pants, one working on the seat and the other on the knees.

How long has it been since you were on your knees before God?

Finally, if you're serious about resisting the devil, always run from trouble. Not long ago, an all-American, college football player visited our church. He played for one of the top five programs in the nation and was a second-round pick in the NFL. I learned later from talking to his uncle that his legs were insured for $1 million. Obviously, he felt that his future depended on his legs.

But then, that's true of everybody!

In his book *Love, Sex, and Lasting Relationships*, Chip Ingram makes a terrific point. He says that God didn't set up boundaries so we could see how close we can get to them without sinning. Rather, he intended for us to see those boundaries and then run as fast as we can in the other direction.[1] This seems to be the mistake a lot of Christians are making. We see a boundary and we say, "That's how far I can go." What we should be saying is, "I'm getting too close to trouble. I need to get out of here."

Solomon reinforces this idea in the book of Proverbs. Referring to an immoral woman, he says, "Run from her! Don't go near the door of her house!" (5:8). Then, a few chapters later, he hits the same idea from the opposite direction: "The name of the LORD is a strong fortress; the godly run to him and are safe" (18:10).

You may have skinny legs or fat legs or bowlegs or beautiful legs. Whatever kind of legs you have, you need to take care of them, because one of these days they may be the only thing standing between you and a catastrophic defeat at the hands of Satan.

Not long ago there was an item on the local news about a man who got up one morning and staggered into his kitchen to put on a pot of coffee. He was still rubbing the sleep out of his eyes when he looked down and saw a three-foot alligator in the middle of the kitchen floor. Apparently, the reptile had entered the house through the doggy door that the man had recently installed. After the authorities removed the gator, the man's first order of business was to get rid of the doggy door.

I couldn't help thinking about Satan when I heard that story. He doesn't need a large opening to gain access to your heart. You can lock all the doors and windows, and he'll simply slip in through the doggy door while you're not looking. That's why every access point must be sealed up tight. Otherwise you greatly increase your chances of ending up in a grave that some future traveler will have to step over.

Dealing with the Dead

But even if you succeed in resisting the devil, there's still the issue of the graves that are already there. Since you will be stepping over a lot of them on your hard-road journey, it's critical that you have the proper mind-set. Let me offer two exhortations.

*First, don't let the graves **deceive** you.* You could become so focused on those who died on your hard road that you begin to believe nobody ever makes it through.

I have a female friend who worked in an office with four other women. All four of them were divorced and bitter about it. As you would expect, my friend had to listen to their negative talk on a daily basis. They compared scars, swapped horror stories, and bashed every male in sight. So what do you think happened when my friend's marriage faced its first big challenge? You guessed it. She was instantly ready to file for divorce without even making a token effort to work things out. When I asked why she was in such a rush to dump her husband, she said, "What's the point of dragging it out? Guys are all alike. He'll never change."

I didn't need a degree in rocket science to figure out what her problem was. For months she'd been spending eight hours a day sitting beside the graves of her coworkers' dead marriages. Their daily rants against men and marriage had so filled her mind with negativity that there wasn't a square inch left for anything positive. Without realizing it, she had been brainwashed into believing that marriage is a stupid idea and that all men are pigs.

The first thing I did was to hook her up with two people who had worked through some serious problems of their own and still managed to build a dynamic relationship. My goal, of course, was to show her that some troubled marriages *don't* end in divorce. I wanted her to see that some couples who face hard roads manage not only to survive, but to thrive. Thankfully, she got the message and committed to counseling. I'm happy to report that her efforts were rewarded, and she and her husband are now very happy together. (By the way, she also found another job. To this day she says that escaping the negativity that filled her former office like thick cigarette smoke was the single most important step she took on behalf of her marriage.)

My friend, as you step over the dead on your hard-road journey, don't be deceived. It might seem as if no one ever survives the road you're traveling, but that's never true. The world is full of survivors. Seek them out and listen to their stories.

*Second, don't let the graves **demoralize** you.* Over the years, I've performed countless graveside services. I've tromped through cemeteries all over the country and read the names, dates, and epitaphs on a thousand headstones. I wonder . . . is there any such thing as a headstone with a happy story behind it? I doubt it.

Recently, I saw a headstone that had these words below the name:

Our beloved son.
Sadly missed.
1986–1997

Instantly my heart felt heavy. The boy had been only eleven years old. Was he killed in an accident? Did he have a disease? Was he murdered? I don't know. But I know that little boys aren't supposed to die at eleven. Therefore, I have to believe that whatever happened was bad. Really bad. I couldn't help wondering if his parents were somewhere in our community, still grieving after all these years.

That's the thing about graves. They'll get you down if you focus on them.

So don't.

Instead, raise your chin and lift up your eyes. Paul said, "Set your sights on the realities of heaven, where Christ sits at God's right hand in the place of honor and power. Let heaven fill your thoughts" (Col. 3:1–2). The apostle understood that a downward gaze leads to trouble. He also knew that nothing is more invigorating than thoughts of heaven.

Before I started writing books, I did quite a few concerts as a saxophonist and vocalist. One of my favorite numbers to perform was a jazzy, swing arrangement of the old hymn "Mansion over the Hilltop." The chorus says:

> I've got a mansion just over the hilltop
> In that bright land where we'll never grow old
> And some day yonder we will never more wander
> But walk on streets that are purest gold.[2]

One night I was singing that song in a church. Lots of folks were tapping their feet and singing along, but one lady near the front was sitting with her face in her hands, and it looked for all the world as though she was weeping. Now, I'll be the first to admit that my singing isn't anything to write home about, but I'd never had anybody break down in tears over it. I watched the lady out of the corner of my eye for the rest of the concert, and I could tell something major was going on inside her. She dabbed her eyes with a tissue and blew her nose numerous times.

As soon as the concert ended, I got the scoop. She came straight over to me and told me how she'd been in an emotional funk for weeks because of some personal problems. She said she was a Christian, but that she'd completely lost sight of God's goodness and His promises—until she heard the chorus of "Mansion over the Hilltop." She said that like a bolt out of the blue, it hit her: As a believer, she had every reason in the world to be happy and hopeful, regardless of her problems.

I will never forget that night. I was deeply moved by her words and reminded once again of how important it is to walk with your chin raised and your eyes lifted up. Dear reader, if you're a Christian, you also have a luxury condo on the beach just over the hilltop. Someday you, too, are going to be walking (not to mention dancing) on streets of purest gold. So don't let the graves along your hard road deceive you. And above all, don't let them demoralize you. Just step over them and keep going.

The LORD *spread out a cloud above them as a covering and gave them a great fire to light the darkness. They asked for meat, and he sent them quail; he gave them manna—bread from heaven. He opened up a rock, and water gushed out to form a river through the dry and barren land. For he remembered his sacred promise to Abraham his servant.*

—PSALM 105:39–42

STRATEGY #6

Trust God to Meet Your Needs

They will survive through hard times;
even in famine they will have more than enough.

—PSALM 37:19

I'm a sucker for any store that has a shelf of used books or records. Even if the place is a dump, I'll go in and look around. (In fact, the dumpiest places have yielded some of my most cherished treasures!) Marilyn often says that I'll cut across six lanes of speeding traffic if I spot a thrift store on the other side of the road. People think she's joking, but she isn't. Considering the number of times I've forced her to hold on for dear life, I'm surprised her handprints aren't pressed into the dash of our car.

One day I was digging through a stack of about twenty-five books in one of my favorite central Florida haunts. It contained quite a few espionage thrillers, a nice collection of westerns, and a few Civil War books. Some macho guy's collection, I assumed, judging from the testosterone in the titles.

And then I found it.

At the very bottom of the pile.

A book that seemed terribly out of place.

71

A book that possessed no testosterone whatsoever.

A book that would deeply impact my life.

It was a book by Elisabeth Elliot titled *A Chance to Die: The Life and Legacy of Amy Carmichael*. I knew that Amy Carmichael had been a missionary and a prolific writer. I had used quite a few quotations from her books over the years. And I knew that she had lived a difficult life. But it wasn't until I read Ms. Elliot's book that I realized what an extraordinary person she was. I am still of the opinion that Amy Carmichael might have walked the hardest road any human (other than Christ) has ever walked.

She lived during the early 1900s and spent the last fifty-five years of her life in Dohnavur, India, rescuing little girls who were doomed by the Hindu religion to serve as temple prostitutes. In all, more than a thousand children, most of whom were orphans, were liberated, cared for, and taught about Jesus as a direct result of her tireless efforts. It's little wonder that they came to call her "Amma," which means "mother" in the Tamil language.

But that doesn't tell even half the story.

While Amy Carmichael was working long hours under difficult conditions, she was suffering as few people ever have. At a time when medical care was primitive at best, she suffered a wide array of physical ailments. Severe headaches tortured her almost daily. A bad heart sapped her strength. Chronic insomnia made it impossible for her to get the rest she needed. Increasing blindness hindered her mobility and contributed to accidents that broke her bones and permanently injured her spine. Eventually she became so feeble that she was confined to her bed, where she spent the last twenty years of her life.

But even that wasn't the worst that would happen.

Shortly before her death, Amy Carmichael fell in the bathroom and so severely injured herself that she couldn't walk, sit, stand, or kneel. She was literally pinned to her back. But even then, she didn't despair. This incredible woman of faith believed that her predicament surely held some sort of lesson to be learned, some critical truth that might help not only her but others who were walking the hard roads of life.

Suddenly, one day, it came to her.

In a moment of insight, she envisioned Jesus on the cross. Not in the upright position we usually picture in our minds, but flat on the ground, on his back, as the nails were being driven into His hands and feet. It was the same position she found herself in, which meant that she was only visiting a place where Jesus had already been. The very idea bathed her in comfort. Later, she said to her friends, "I tell you this because some of you may find yourselves in hard ways. Always, your Lord has been before you. Always, he will come with a most heavenly understanding of what your heart most needs."[1]

That is the simple message of this chapter and one of the most important in this book. Our Lord is "acquainted with bitterest grief" (Isa. 53:3). He knows every twist and turn in the hardest roads we have to travel and, therefore, understands what we will need to make it through.

Again, the Israelites are the perfect example.

Even as He banished them to the wilderness for a forty-year hike, God knew they'd never make it without His help. So, in spite of their rebellion, He went along with them, patiently and lovingly providing for their needs. When they needed direction, He provided a pillar of fire for the night and a cloud for the day. When they needed water, He cracked open a rock and sent it gushing out. And when they needed food, which was every single day, He provided manna.

A Closer Look at the Manna

Over the years, manna has been the symbol of choice when people talk about the faithfulness of God in meeting the needs of His children. Numbers 11 tells us that it came down with the dew during the night (v. 9), looked like coriander seeds (v. 7), was pale yellow in color (v. 7), and was ground into flour to make flat cakes (v. 8). Beyond that, there are three things we know about the manna that should give every hard-road traveler a lot of comfort.

First, the manna was never too early and never too late. I can appreciate this because my copy of the *Orlando Sentinel* is supposed to be delivered by six o'clock every morning. When I step out of my house at about seven, it's supposed to be lying on my driveway. And most of the time it is. But occasionally it isn't. And I tell you, it never fails. Those mornings when it isn't there always seem to be the mornings when I'm especially anxious to read about a big news story or to tear into the sports page and get the scores from the night before.

It should encourage every hard-road traveler to know that there was never a morning when the Israelites went out to gather their manna and came back empty-handed. When their stomachs were growling, it was there, waiting to be picked up.

But this shouldn't surprise us. Isaiah 30:23 says, "The LORD will bless you with rain at planting time." Not at harvest time, but at planting time when the need is critical. In other words, friend, you can relax and trust God to provide *what* you need *when* you need it.

Second, the manna was never too much and never too little. There is a restaurant in Orlando that offers a thirty-two-ounce steak on its menu. I don't know if you've ever seen a thirty-two-ounce steak, but it's roughly the size of a Ford Focus. And here's the kicker: If you can manage to choke down all thirty-two ounces, your meal is free. I know a guy who did it once. I say once because it made him sick, and he swore he'd never do it again. Too much food is not a good thing.

But neither is too little food.

A lack of nutrition can cause everything from lethargy and hair loss to anemia, brittle bones, premature births, and a host of life-threatening diseases. The life expectancy in many third-world countries doesn't exceed fifty years, primarily because of a lack of good nutrition.

So God made sure that His people had enough manna, but not too much. Exodus 16:21 says, "The people gathered the food morning by morning, *each family according to its need*" (emphasis added). In other words, even if you were like the old woman who lived in a shoe, you never faced a shortage. But neither did you have a storage problem, because any manna that wasn't picked up melted in the growing heat of the morning sun (16:21).

So we see that not only is God's timing always perfect in meeting our needs, but so are His measurements. If you are traveling a hard road, you can relax and trust God to provide as much as you will need to make it through.

Third, the manna was never too hard and never too easy. Not long ago I saw one of our middle school boys working on his math homework in the church fellowship hall. When I saw that he was using a calculator, I said, "Hey, isn't that cheating?" He quickly informed me that not only was it permissible to use a calculator, but his teacher actually encouraged it. Suddenly I felt cheated! When I was in school, we had to do the calculations in our heads. (Or on our fingers and toes!) Why, if I had had a calculator in those days, I might not have had to rely so much on my apple-polishing ability in order to pass!

Yes, easy is good. We love easy.

But it's not good if things are too easy.

I keep reading that achievement test scores in our schools are declining. Could it be because we are making things too easy for our kids? Would we perhaps be better off if we actually taught our kids how to do math instead of teaching them how to work a calculator?

Here again, we see that God struck the perfect balance with His people. Yes, the manna showed up on the ground right on time every morning. It was, in essence, delivered to their front doors. But they still had some work to do. They had to gather it, grind it, and bake it. Yes, God was feeding them, but He wasn't spoon-feeding them.

And He won't spoon-feed you, either—even if you are on a hard road.

Why? Because He knows that when we work together with Him, we grow into a deeper relationship with Him. And that, ultimately, is what He wants. Yes, your physical welfare is a concern to Him, but your spiritual welfare is an even higher priority. In other words, yes, He wants to keep you *going*. But even more, He wants to keep you *growing*. He desperately wants to bond with you and develop a relationship that will last far beyond the end of your hard road.

A Closer Look at the Master

These truths about the manna only serve to deepen my love and appreciation for God. They force me to contemplate His faithfulness and character, and the more I do, the more confidence I have that He will take care of me.

Charles Haddon Spurgeon, the great nineteenth-century preacher, spent more than twenty years writing *The Treasury of David*, a seven-volume commentary on the book of Psalms that has long been considered a classic. By comparison, the book you're holding in your hands took me about one year to write, so I can't even fathom spending twenty years on a project. But he did, and the reason he never grew tired of it was because the Psalms are so rich in truth. (Hence the word *treasury* in his title.) Almost every day he gained an exciting new insight about God. Here's one of my favorites, taken from his comments on Psalm 23, which begins, "The LORD is my Shepherd . . ."

> The sweetest word of the whole is that monosyllable, "my." He does not say, "The Lord is the shepherd of the world at large, and leadeth forth the multitude as his flock." If he is a shepherd to no one else, he is a shepherd to me. He cares for me, watches over me, and preserves me. The words are in the present tense. Whatever be the believer's position, he is even now under the pastoral care of Jehovah.[2]

This is precisely what every hard-road traveler needs to understand and believe. God never loses anyone in the shuffle. Though the world is full of needy people, no one ever slips through the cracks. If you're living in the heart of a crowded city, or stranded in a remote corner of the planet, don't worry. God is still your Shepherd. He sees you, He knows what you need, and He will provide.

Eddie Rickenbacker, easily one of the most colorful characters in American history, came to understand this very well. He was a World War I flying ace who downed twenty-six enemy aircraft, a designer and builder of his own line of automobiles, one of the very first race-car drivers, and the owner and operator of the Indianapolis Speedway for twenty years. He also survived two plane crashes, the second of which set him on a particularly hard road.

The year was 1942. Eddie was asked by the secretary of war to deliver a message to General Douglas MacArthur, who was headquartered at Port Moresby, New Guinea, in the South Pacific. The message was so sensitive that it couldn't be put on paper, so it was given to Eddie orally and he committed it to memory. On the night of October 18, he took off with a crew of eight from an airbase in Hawaii, not realizing that he was embarking on perhaps the most incredible adventure of his already amazing life.

The flight required a circuitous route, because the Japanese controlled the waters in a straight line between Hawaii and New Guinea. That, along with a slight navigational error and a stronger-than-anticipated tailwind, caused the plane to overshoot the island that was their destination. Before they realized what was happening, they found themselves so far from land that they didn't have enough fuel to get back. The only option they had was to ditch the plane in the middle of the ocean.

The pilot managed to get the plane down safely, and it stayed afloat until all the men could climb aboard the two rafts that no one believed they'd ever have to use. At that point they were all alive, but facing three enormous problems. The first was that they had left their water and rations on the plane. All they had between them were a dozen chocolate bars and a few oranges. Their second problem was that they had no idea where they were. And the third—and by far their biggest problem—was that no one else knew where they were either. They were certain that military aircraft would be dispatched to search for them, but they were equally certain that those planes would be looking in all the wrong places.

This, of course, was not the first time Eddie Rickenbacker had stared death in the face. He was actually quite experienced at it, so the rest of the men allowed him to assume control of the situation. Immediately he set up a system of two-hour watches so there would be eyes on the water and the skies at all times. Then he formulated a schedule for eating the oranges and candy bars. Finally, he determined that they would pray together twice a day, morning and evening.

One of the men had a small New Testament in his pocket, so it wasn't long before their little prayer times turned into full-blown worship services. They would pass the little Bible around, find their favorite Scriptures to read aloud, and sing the hymns they had learned as boys in Sunday school. They couldn't always remember the words, but they sang anyway, often at the tops of their lungs, as if to scare away the demons that were hovering overhead and waiting to steal their hope.

It was on their eighth day at sea that something amazing happened.

The men were desperately hungry and spent a good bit of their prayer time pleading for God's mercy. When they finished, Eddie settled back in the raft and pulled his cap over his face to shield his eyes from the sun. He'd just dozed off when he felt something land on his head. He couldn't see it, but somehow he knew it was a seagull. All of the men froze and no one said a word. The last thing they wanted to do was to scare it away. They knew that if they could somehow catch it, they could eat.

Ever so slowly, a fraction of an inch at a time, Eddie moved his trembling hand toward the bird. Again, he couldn't see it, but he painted a mental image of where it would be, judging from the pressure on his head. Excruciating seconds passed as his hand slowly moved into position. The men held their breaths and prayed like never before. Then, in a flash, Eddie grabbed for the bird, caught it by the feet, and hung on for dear life. Its fluttering wings kicked up a tornado of dancing feathers, but there would be no escape.

In minutes, the bird was defeathered and cut into eight equal pieces. The men chewed the tough, sinewy meat slowly, bones and all, and felt that it was the finest-tasting meal they'd ever enjoyed.

And they were just getting started.

When they finished eating, they rigged a fishing line and used the bird's intestines for bait. In no time, one of the men landed a twelve-inch mackerel, and then Eddie himself pulled in a sea bass. In a matter of minutes, they went from being half-dead from starvation to fully alive with bulging stomachs.

And that's not all.

That very night, it rained for the first time since the crash. The men caught the water in their bailing buckets and lay back with their mouths open to catch as much as they could. Eddie would remark later that nothing ever tasted so good, before or since.[3]

Was it just a coincidence that all of these good things started happening within five minutes after the men finished pleading for God's mercy? One could almost believe so, except for one thing: The bird was hundreds of miles from land. What seagull flies hundreds of miles straight out into the middle of the ocean, unless it's keeping a divine appointment?

Right now you're probably not floating on a raft, starving to death in the middle of the Pacific Ocean. But you're probably adrift in your own personal sea of anguish, or you wouldn't have progressed so far into this book. The road you're traveling is probably, in its own way, as difficult as the one on which Eddie Rickenbacker and his crew found themselves.

If so, take a closer look at our wonderful God.

He is El Shaddai, the all-sufficient God. He is the maker of manna and the sender of seagulls. In Psalm 139:7–10, David nailed it. He said:

> I can never escape from your spirit! I can never get away from your presence! If I go up to heaven, you are there; if I go down to the place of the dead, you are there. If I ride the wings of the morning,

if I dwell by the farthest oceans, even there your hand will guide me, and your strength will support me.

One of my favorite hymns says:

> No matter what may be the test,
> God will take care of you;
> Lean, weary one, upon His breast,
> God will take care of you.[4]

At a time in your life when you're probably feeling overwhelmed with bad news, this is the good news. No, this is the *best* news. Wherever your hard road takes you, God will be there, and He will take care of you.

As I come to the end of this chapter, it's February 1, 2004. The sun isn't up yet, but it's casting a faint orange glow in the eastern sky. I know this day won't hold any special significance for a lot of people. They'll bounce out of bed and go about their business as usual. But for some, it's going to be very painful. You see, it was one year ago today that the space shuttle *Columbia* broke apart and exploded while reentering the earth's atmosphere, instantly killing all seven crew members and launching their families and loved ones on one of the hardest roads a human being can travel.

The reason this is on my mind is because I have been reading Evelyn Husband's book, *High Calling*. Her husband, Rick, was the shuttle commander and a devout Christian. Inside the book there are some photographs, and one in particular has held me captive. I have found myself looking at it again and again. It shows Evelyn, along with her children, Laura and Matthew, waiting for the shuttle to land. They are all smiles, and in the background you can see the countdown clock, showing eleven minutes and twenty-one seconds until touchdown. What they do not know is that the shuttle has already exploded. Literally seconds after the picture was snapped, they learned the news that would change their lives forever.

Isn't it amazing how quickly a person's world can come crashing down?

Smiles can turn to sobs in no time flat.

But I love this book. *High Calling* has ministered to me, especially as I have been working on this chapter. It has reassured me that the words I am putting on these pages are not just motivational psychobabble. They are true, and they are being proved so every day in the lives of real people. People like Evelyn Husband. Read her words carefully, and let them nourish your hurting soul.

> I have lost all sense of politeness with God. I have cried and wept and yelled at Him, but I know He's big enough to handle it. He has drawn me closer than I ever thought possible. He has held me close to His heart and let me cry for as long as I've needed. My sweet sister-in-law, Kathy, told me on February 1 that God would walk me step-by-step through this sorrow, and He has. Time and again, what the Lord said in the Bible has proved faithful and true.[5]

I don't know of anyone who would be more qualified to speak to the issue of God's faithfulness to hard-road travelers than Evelyn Husband. Others may wonder, but she, of all people, knows His promises are true.

And what He's doing for her, He will do for you.

Trust Him to meet your needs.

When the cloud lifted from over the sacred tent, the people of Israel followed it. And wherever the cloud settled, the people of Israel camped. In this way, they traveled at the LORD's command and stopped wherever he told them to. Then they remained where they were as long as the cloud stayed over the Tabernacle. If the cloud remained over the Tabernacle for a long time, the Israelites stayed for a long time, just as the LORD commanded. Sometimes the cloud would stay over the Tabernacle for only a few days, so the people would stay for only a few days. Then at the LORD's command they would break camp. Sometimes the cloud stayed only overnight and moved on the next morning. But day or night, when the cloud lifted, the people broke camp and followed. Whether the cloud stayed above the Tabernacle for two days, a month, or a year, the people of Israel stayed in camp and did not move on. But as soon as it lifted, they broke camp and moved on. So they camped or traveled at the LORD's command, and they did whatever the LORD told them through Moses.

—NUMBERS 9:17–23

Go at God's Pace

But these things I plan won't happen right away.
Slowly, steadily, surely, the time approaches when the
vision will be fulfilled. If it seems slow, wait patiently,
for it will surely take place.

—HABAKKUK 2:3

On April 16, 1846, a large, well-equipped wagon train rolled out of Springfield, Illinois, and headed for California. The leaders of that expedition, George and Jacob Donner, had read Lansford Hastings's book, *The Emigrant's Guide to Oregon and California*, and were captivated by his portrayal of California as a sort of second Eden. Even though they were wealthy men who were well established in Illinois, they felt that the trip west would lead them to even greater prosperity.

They were also inspired by Hastings's report of a new shortcut that would veer off from the established route at Fort Bridger, cut through the Wasatch Mountains, and save them hundreds of miles. What they didn't realize (and Hastings failed to mention) was that no one had ever actually traveled the shortcut to make sure it was passable.

When the wagon train reached Fort Bridger, it was decision time. Some of the more conservative souls chose to stick with the original route that hundreds of wagons had already traveled successfully. But eighty-seven men, women, and children, including George and Jacob Donner, decided to take what had become known as the Hastings Cutoff. That decision would lead them into a nightmare of unspeakable proportions.

At first the going was easy and spirits were high. But in time, the trail dwindled away to nothing. In some places, they found themselves having to hack through thick underbrush just to move the wagons inches at a time. They also encountered an eighty-mile stretch of desert that caused many of their animals to die of thirst. And worst of all, they were unable to make the final pull over the Sierras because their remaining animals were too weak and malnourished.

When the winter snows came, they had no choice but to hunker down and try to survive the winter. But that was easier said than done. Temperatures dropped below freezing, and food supplies quickly ran out.

In desperation, the settlers decided that one of them should die so the others could live. It was agreed that lots would be cast and the loser would be killed to provide food for the others. Slips of paper were prepared and distributed, and the fatal slip was drawn by a man named Patrick Dolan. But in the end, no one had the heart to kill him. About half the people eventually did resort to cannibalism as first one person and then another froze or starved to death, but only after eating rawhide, leather scraps, bones, and whatever else they could find.

Eventually, two rescue expeditions were able to reach the survivors and lead them on to California. Of the eighty-seven members of what is now known as the Donner Party, forty-one died, including every member of the two Donner families. Virginia Reed was an adolescent who managed to survive the ordeal, and when she got to California, she wrote the following words to her cousin back east:

> Oh, Mary. I have not wrote you half of the trouble we've had, but I have wrote you enough to let you know what trouble is. But thank God, we are the only family that did not eat human flesh. We have left everything, but I don't care for that. We have got through with our lives. Don't let this letter dishearten anybody. Remember, never take no cutoffs . . .[1]

People love a shortcut. As flies to honey, we're drawn to anything that looks as though it could be faster and easier. And that's often a good thing. Our need for speed has taken us all the way from covered wagons to supersonic transportation. And now, instead of cooking our food over an open fire, we merely need to touch a button on our microwaves. But as the story of the Donner Party painfully illustrates, thoughtless hurrying can get you into a lot of trouble.

We know that the Israelites were condemned to a forty-year journey through the wilderness. So in a sense, there was no reason to hurry. Yet the Bible reveals the intriguing fact that God stopped them in various places along the way, sometimes for as long as a year (Num. 9:22). And we know that some of those campsites were more pleasant than others. For example, some had plenty of water, while others had little. I can only imagine how antsy they must have become when they found themselves in a less-than-ideal location. The temptation to pack up and move on ahead of God's prompting must have been very powerful. I'm sure there were even times, especially during the latter years of the wandering period, when they felt like chucking the wilderness altogether and making a mad dash for the Promised Land. But if they'd done that, they would have suffered even more.

Your Big Challenge

As a hard-road traveler, you're no doubt feeling a strong tempta-tion to try to hurry things along. Believing that the end of your painful road is out there somewhere, you naturally want to hurry up and get there. (Who wouldn't?) But if you're not careful, Satan will use your sense of urgency against you.

Just ask April.

She was an attractive, thirty-four-year-old single mother whose road through life was being made hard by three kids under the age of seven, an eight-dollar-an-hour job, a ten-year-old car that needed a major engine overhaul, and an ex-husband who always had enough money to wine and dine his twenty-two-year-old girlfriend but never enough to pay his child support.

One day she met a man who was doing consulting work for her employer. He was fifteen years her senior, but very handsome and obviously well-to-do. He took an immediate interest in her and, amazingly, seemed not to be bothered by the fact that she had three young children. They immediately started dating, and within two months, a proposal was on the table. April knew it was too soon to get married. She barely knew the man. But she had been praying that God would bring someone into her life, so it was easy for her to convince herself that this man was the answer to her prayers and the solution to her problems.

He wasn't.

Within days after the wedding ceremony, the outbursts of anger started. At first, he merely raised his voice, which was something he'd never done while they were dating. Then he started punching and throwing things. The marriage lasted less than a year, and April was left with even more wounds—both physical and emotional—than she'd had before she met him.

I do not stand in judgment of April. I think anybody in her situation would have been tempted to do exactly what she did. Her story simply illustrates the challenge all hard-road travelers face. You simply must find a way to slow down when every fiber of your being is screaming, "Hurry up!" Let me offer three suggestions that will make slowing down a little easier for you.

First, reflect on life's lessons regarding the importance of slowing down. Bad things happen every day because people fail to tap the brakes when they should. And sometimes the results are catastrophic.

On January 28, 1986, the space shuttle *Challenger* exploded shortly after takeoff. Naturally, there was a full-scale investigation, and what it revealed was shocking. Scientists had noticed a problem with the shuttle's O-rings, which were ultimately identified as the cause of the explosion. The launch should have been postponed and the O-ring problem fixed, but NASA foolishly charged ahead and launched the spaceship anyway. Why? Because President Reagan was to deliver his State of the Union address on the very night of the launch and planned to talk about Christa McAuliffe and the teacher-in-space program that had put her on board. It was to be a glorious moment for NASA. The whole nation would be watching. The last thing NASA wanted was for the shuttle to be sitting on the launching pad with mechanical problems.

Correction . . .

The *second* to last thing NASA wanted was for the shuttle to be sitting on the launching pad with mechanical problems.

The *last* thing they wanted was a midair explosion.

I've heard it said that sometimes life whispers her lessons and sometimes, as on January 28, 1986, she screams them. Sadly, some people still never hear what she's trying to tell them. Don't be one of them. Pay attention to the lessons of history.

*Second, slowing down will be easier if you **remember** what you have been called to do.* Micah 6:8 says it very succinctly: "This is what [the Lord] requires: to do what is right, to love mercy, and to *walk humbly with your God*" (emphasis added). There are three words in that last phrase that are worth noting.

The first one is *walk*. We are to walk with God.

One of the reasons I don't jog is because all the joggers I see look as though they're in agony. Their faces are twisted into the sort of grotesque expressions one might see on a person who's having surgery—without anesthesia! I figure life is too short to put myself through that kind of torture. I prefer instead to walk. I don't cover as much ground as quickly as a runner, but I do eventually get where I'm going and, judging from those facial expressions, I'm quite confident that I enjoy the trip a lot more.

I love the fact that God is a walker and not a runner. I'm sure I wouldn't be able to keep up if He were racing through my circumstances at breakneck speed. Even now I sometimes grow weary and fall behind in getting to where I know God wants me to be. If I had to run, I'm sure I'd never make it.

The second word I want you to think about in Micah 6:8 is *with*. We are to walk *with* God.

Marilyn and I love to walk together, but we have a hard time staying together. My stride is longer, so naturally I have a tendency to pull ahead of her. That problem is compounded if we happen to be heading for something I'm passionate about. One time we were walking toward Busch Stadium for a Cardinals game and I heard someone calling my name. I turned around and there she was, a good fifteen feet behind me, breathing hard, weaving through the crowd, and trying unsuccessfully to keep up with me. I had become so obsessed with getting inside the stadium to see Mark McGwire take batting practice that I practically ran off and left her!

We can do the same thing with God if we aren't careful. When we get excited, we can thoughtlessly charge on ahead and leave Him to eat our dust. That's why there are so many admonitions in Scripture like Lamentations 3:25: "The LORD is wonderfully good to those who wait for him."

And then there's the word *humbly*. We are to walk humbly with God.

The other day in a shopping mall I saw a woman marching down the walkway as if she was on a mission. Struggling to keep up was a skinny little man carrying her bags and packages. As they walked, she barked an order: "Sit down on that bench while I go into this store!" The man dutifully took a seat, panting, and awaited her return. When she came out, she said, "Come on. Let's go!" and started beating feet. The little man, who was obviously her husband, frantically grabbed their stuff and took off after her.

I think we're all sometimes guilty of doing to God what that woman was doing to her husband. We treat Him like a porter—like someone whose only job is to follow us wherever we want to go and carry all of our burdens. Maybe that's why Micah threw that word *humbly* into the mix. It's a not-so-subtle reminder of God's authority. Yes, we are invited—even commanded—to walk with Him. But it is never our place to assume control and start dictating the pace and direction of the walk.

And finally, slowing down will be easier if you reject the counsel of people who urge you to hurry up. Not long ago, a young woman came to my office seeking advice. Her husband had admitted to having a sexual encounter with a coworker. He seemed repentant and expressed a desire to save the marriage. The woman, though deeply hurt and apprehensive, felt inclined to give it a try. However, her friends and a few of her family members were urging her to dump him and move on. They questioned whether she'd ever be able to trust him again and assured her that she was young and attractive enough to find someone a lot better.

With all of these voices ringing in her ears, the woman became thoroughly confused and asked what I thought she should do. I told her it was a no-brainer. God wanted her to do everything in her power to save the marriage. Dumping her husband might provide a quick fix, but it wouldn't glorify God. Nor would it set a good example for others who might be struggling. But slowing down, seeking wise counsel, and patiently working through their issues would give God an opportunity to do a mighty work.

I'm happy to report that the marriage was saved, and the couple are happier than ever before. The following is a portion of a letter she sent me:

> I know my family meant well. But I shudder to think where I would have been and what I would have missed if I had taken their advice. Thank you for reminding me not to seek quick fixes, but to do things God's way, even if it's more painful. It's a lesson I will teach my children.

There are obviously times when it's appropriate to hurry. But when someone—even someone you love—urges you to act impulsively, you need to be very careful. Remember that the decision you make will probably not affect the people who are so freely offering you advice. But it could profoundly affect you, possibly for years to come.

Your Big Chance

Right now, you could well be at one of the most critical points in your hard-road journey. You have a chance to tap into the deepest reservoirs of God's strength if you can find a way to slow down and wait for the impulses of His Spirit. The following words should be highlighted in every hard-road traveler's Bible:

> Those who wait on the LORD will find new strength. They will fly high on wings like eagles. They will run and not grow weary. They will walk and not faint. (Isa. 40:31)

Eagles are amazing birds. They can actually fly as high as fourteen thousand feet. So high, in fact, that they cannot be seen with the naked eye from the ground. You'd think that in order to accomplish such a feat, they'd have to expend tremendous amounts of energy. But they don't. In fact, they barely flap their wings at all. Instead, they take advantage of thermals.

Simply put, thermals are columns of warm air rising upward from the ground. They're created when one area of the earth's surface, such as an asphalt parking lot, heats up in the morning sun faster than, say, an adjacent grassy field. An eagle will leave his perch, find one of these thermals, and extend his wings. The upward flow of air will push him as high as he wants to go.

I doubt that Isaiah would have been able to explain the science behind thermals, but he obviously observed their effects. He could see that eagles were lifted up and sustained, not by their own efforts, but by some sort of invisible force. It reminded him of the amazing way God lifts and sustains His followers in hard times.

But the key is still our willingness to be patient and wait on

Him. He wants to know that we are trusting in Him and not in our own strength or ingenuity.

A vivid example of this is seen in Isaiah 30. When Assyria threatened to attack, the leaders of Judah did not wait on God. Instead, they got the bright idea of trying to negotiate an alliance with Egypt. Their representatives traveled through a snake-infested wilderness to strike the deal (v. 6), but the plan ultimately failed. Egypt's promises turned out to be worthless (v. 7). Naturally, God was furious, and delivered a stinging rebuke that I want you to read slowly and carefully. And pay special attention to the italicized words:

> The Sovereign LORD, the Holy One of Israel, says, "*Only in returning to me and waiting for me will you be saved. In quietness and confidence is your strength.* But you would have none of it. You said, 'No, we will get our help from Egypt. They will give us swift horses for riding into battle.' But the only swiftness you are going to see is the swiftness of your enemies chasing you! One of them will chase a thousand of you. Five of them will make all of you flee. You will be left like a lonely flagpole on a distant mountaintop." (Isa. 30:15–17, emphasis added)

And then Isaiah adds his own postscript:

> But the LORD still waits for you to come to him so he can show you his love and compassion. For the LORD is a faithful God. *Blessed are those who wait for him to help them.* (v. 18, emphasis added)

I know it's hard.

Life is moving at warp speed.

People are zipping past you at a dead run.

When you hesitate, you get honked at.

When you slow down, you feel you're falling behind.

When you try to relax, you feel guilty.

And when you do nothing, you feel like a bum.

All of this is Satan's attempt to keep you scrambling like mad. He, better than anybody, understands that speed kills. He knows that if he can keep you frantic, he can keep you weak and vulnerable. You see, he knows the Scriptures better than you or I. You may never have thought about that before, but it's true. Satan is the ultimate Bible scholar. He knows every Scripture I've shared with you in this chapter by heart. He fully understands that those who wait on the Lord will gain new strength and soar like eagles.

But now, finally, you understand too.

So turn the tables on him.

Kick off your running shoes and slip into a pair of walkers.

Starting today, the pressure's off.

You can relax . . .

Take a deep breath . . .

And simply walk with the God who loves you.

After leaving Marah, they came to Elim, where there were twelve springs and seventy palm trees. They camped there beside the springs.

—EXODUS 15:27

STRATEGY #8

Enjoy Every Oasis

I will make springs in the desert,
so that my chosen people can be refreshed.

—ISAIAH 43:20

In Exodus 15, shortly after their Red Sea experience, the Israelites entered the Shur Desert and traveled for three days without finding water.

I can't imagine how they must have felt.

When my throat gets dry, I simply grab my favorite insulated glass and head for the refrigerator. By pressing it against a couple of levers, I can fill it with cubes (or crushed ice if I'm feeling sassy) and top it off with a stream of crisp, filtered water. Or, if I get thirsty when I'm traveling, I just wheel into a convenience store and pick up a bottle of Dasani. In fact, I have a chilled bottle of Dasani sitting beside me as I'm writing these words. Never in my life have I been afraid that I might die of thirst.

But the Israelites were.

One by one, their canteens were hitting empty, the blazing sun was beating down on their tired backs, and after three long days of trudging through the desert, all they could see in every direction was more sand and rock.

Talk about frightening!

But finally, they found water at a place called Marah. The name sounds pretty in English, but they knew all too well that it meant "bitter" or "stagnant," and sure enough, one whiff told them the water wasn't fit to drink. If you've ever smelled stagnant water, you know that it ranks right up there with dirty diapers and rotten meat. Not surprisingly, the sickening stench pushed them over the edge emotionally. The last of their courage melted away, and panic started blowing through the camp like the first chill of winter. Not knowing what else to do, the people cried out to Moses, who, in turn, cried out to God.

And, as usual, God saved the day.

He ordered Moses to pick up a branch and toss it into the murky pool. Miraculously, the water became sweeter than any the Culligan Man could produce, and the people were able to drink all they wanted, water their livestock, and refill their canteens. I wouldn't be surprised if there was a fair amount of frolicking as well. I can picture both the adults and the children refreshing themselves by splashing around in the crystal-clear water.

But if they enjoyed Marah, the Israelites must have really had a ball at the next stop. Exodus 15:27 says that they came to a place called Elim, where there were twelve springs (one for each of the tribes) and seventy palm trees.

It was a full-blown oasis.

In case you're wondering, oases are created when seismic shifts beneath the surface of the earth interrupt the normal flow of underground springs and push the water to the surface. They can be large and fertile enough to support an entire agricultural community or small enough to offer little more than a drink of water and some shade. I'm told that walking out of the desert and into a large oasis feels a lot like walking into an air-conditioned room. The drop in temperature can be as much as twenty degrees.

On the surface, it might seem odd that Exodus 15:27 was even included in Scripture. After all, there's no action or drama in it. Neither God nor Moses does or says anything remarkable. But don't be fooled. Exodus 15:27 is loaded with significance. It is the hard-road traveler's reminder that oases are real.

Maybe you're just getting started on your hard road and you're deeply discouraged. Perhaps your first steps have been agonizingly difficult and you feel you're not going to be able to endure. Well, cheer up! Every desert has some oases, and sooner or later you're going to come to one. It's true! Even on the hardest roads, there are wonderful pleasures to be found. Here are four sources of refreshment you can enjoy along the way.

Refreshing Seasons

During the Vietnam War, John McCain was a naval aviator who flew combat missions behind enemy lines. In 1967, his plane was hit over Hanoi. He ejected, parachuted to the ground, and was immediately picked up by the Vietnamese. When they discovered that both his father and grandfather had been four-star admirals in the U.S. Navy, they offered to release him. McCain, however, refused. There is a long-standing protocol that prisoners of war should be released in the order of their capture, and he knew there were many other soldiers who'd been held a lot longer. He simply couldn't bring himself to "cut the line" and walk out ahead of them.

So, for the next five years he was held prisoner. He was tortured and often held in solitary confinement. Yet even in such a nightmarish situation, there were still some seasons of refreshing. For example, at Christmastime in 1970, McCain was taken to a large room in the "Hanoi Hilton" where he was united with other captured pilots, their crewmen, and prisoners from other camps. The place was quickly dubbed "Camp Unity" as the men pulled together and shared their strength and their hope. Read McCain's words carefully, and pay special attention to the second paragraph:

> That first night, when so many of us were unexpectedly allowed one another's company, not a single man slept. We talked all night and well into the next day. We talked about everything. What might this change in our fortunes mean? Were we going home soon? Had the Vietnamese some public relations reason for putting us together? Had they been embarrassed by some new disclosure of their abusive treatment of us? We talked about what we had endured at the hands of the enemy; about the escapes some men had attempted and the consequences they suffered as a result. We talked about news from home. We talked about our families, and the lives we hoped to return to soon.
>
> No other experience in my life could ever replicate my first night in Camp Unity, and the feeling of relief that overcame me to be living among my friends. I have lived many happy years since, and am a blessed and contented man. But I will never experience again the supreme happiness I felt my fourth Christmas in Hanoi.[1]

I'll bet you never thought the "supreme happiness" of a man's life could happen in a prison, half a world away from his family and loved ones. But for John McCain it did. Even on that most barren of roads, he found an oasis, a season of refreshing that he will remember the rest of his life.

And you will too.

You may not think so now, but you will experience seasons of sweet relief. Solomon said that there is a time to cry and a time to laugh, a time to grieve and a time to dance (Eccl. 3:4). Those times of laughing and dancing may be few and far between, and they may come when you least expect them, but they will come. And when they do, you need to enjoy them.

Not long ago, I was walking through our local Publix supermarket and ran into one of our church members, a lady who's been fighting a difficult battle with cancer. I was surprised that she had the strength to be out and commented that she looked wonderful, which she did. She smiled and said, "For the last few days I've really felt good—better than I have in quite a while. I decided I was going to get out and enjoy myself a little. I even went to the mall and did some shopping!"

What a great attitude! She was enjoying a refreshing season.

Refreshing Servants

Sometimes it won't be a change in circumstances that refreshes you, but a special person who comes along at just the right time and offers exactly what you need. In Scripture, I see a wonderful example of this in Exodus 17.

You may recall that the Israelites didn't march out of Egypt empty-handed. Exodus 12:36 says, "The LORD caused the Egyptians to look favorably on the Israelites, and they gave the Israelites whatever they asked for. So, like a victorious army, they plundered the Egyptians!" Miles of precious fabrics and countless items of gold and silver would have been stuffed into the Israelites' luggage as they walked out of the country.

That was the good news.

The bad news was that they made an inviting target for bandits and renegades. Think about it. With 430 years of slavery behind them, they were not experienced fighters and possessed few weapons, yet they were loaded down with valuables. No wonder the warriors of Amalek decided to have a go at them.

The battle was fought at a place called Rephidim, and it's noteworthy because of the way God's power was imparted to His people. Moses positioned himself on top of a nearby hill so he could be seen by those fighting in the valley. When he raised his staff over his head with both hands, the power of God flowed freely and the Israelites gained the advantage. But when he lowered his staff, the Amalekites gained the upper hand.

Have you ever tried to hold your arms over your head for even five minutes? If you have, you know it wasn't long before Moses was suffering big-time. That's when Moses' brother Aaron and an obscure Israelite by the name of Hur stepped forward and offered their assistance. First, they found a stone for Moses to sit on. Then they stood on each side of him and held up his hands until sunset. Keeping that staff in the air enabled the Israelites to crush the warriors of Amalek (Ex. 17:13).

Aaron and Hur were in the right place at the right time and provided just what Moses needed. They refreshed him at a critical moment when fatigue threatened to overcome him. They enabled him to sustain an effort that he otherwise would have been forced to abandon. In other words, they did all the things for him that an oasis would do for a weary desert traveler!

Thankfully, there are many compassionate people in the world who find great joy in refreshing those who are suffering.

I met one of them just this morning.

I stopped at the hospital to visit one of our elderly members who is seriously ill and walked in on an amazing scene. The old gentleman had soiled his clothes and his bed, leaving an awful odor in the air. My initial thought was to flee and come back later. But I was captivated by a pretty young orderly, probably in her middle twenties, who was cleaning things up with a smile and humming a little tune. She stopped long enough to greet me and then did something that brought a lump to my throat. She picked up the old man's hand, held it in both of hers, and said, "This is my new papaw. My real papaw died when I was just a little girl, and I've been looking for one ever since. So we made a deal that Mr. Roberts here is going to be my papaw from now on." And then she looked at him and said, "Isn't that right?" The look on his face was one of absolute joy as he nodded yes.

Somehow, that young woman had managed to turn a very painful and embarrassing moment into a happy one for a sick old man. And I had no doubt that she worked the same magic all day long, up and down the corridor, with every patient she was called on to serve. In fact, I suspected that she had several "papaws" on that floor, and probably a few "mamaws" too.

The experience reminded me of the time my dad had to undergo chemotherapy and radiation for rectal cancer. He'd heard all kinds of horror stories about their devastating side effects, that sometimes the treatments were worse than the cancer itself. So naturally, he was dreading it. However, the people who administered the treatments were so kind, so compassionate, and so upbeat that Dad actually began to enjoy the times he spent with them. When I called home to see how he was coping, he spent a minute or two talking about the treatments and twenty minutes talking about the people. He recounted their funny conversations and passed along the jokes they told him. As he rambled on and on, I silently thanked God for those wonderful people who were, for him, an oasis.

As you travel your hard road, many people will cross your path.

They won't all be a blessing to you, but a few of them will be, even if for only a moment. Give thanks for those refreshing servants, and enjoy the pleasure they bring into your life.

And one more thing before I move on.

Stop and consider that perhaps *you* could be a refreshing servant to some other hard-road traveler. I know you're hurting. I know you probably don't feel you're in any condition to minister to others. Maybe just surviving each day is all you feel you have the strength for right now. But don't forget the promise of Scripture: "Those who refresh others will themselves be refreshed" (Prov. 11:25).

The implication of that verse is staggering.

It means you can make your own oasis!

You don't do it by whining and acting pitiful so people will come and minister to you. You do it by ministering to someone else! Remember, Jesus promised that your gift would return to you in full measure (Luke 6:38). And Paul said you will reap what you sow (Gal. 6:7). Why not give it a try?

Think of someone in your neighborhood, workplace, or church who is staggering through a desert of adversity. Then go out of your way to be an oasis to that person. Don't be loud and flashy about it. In fact, it's probably best if no one even knows what you're up to. Just do it in the name of Jesus. And above all, don't worry about getting a blessing in return. Don't look up to heaven and say, "Okay, God, I refreshed somebody. Now when do *I* get refreshed?" Instead, just keep giving and trust God to keep His word.

He didn't say that those who refresh others *might* be refreshed, or *could* be refreshed, or *should* be refreshed. He said they *will* be refreshed.

You can take it to the bank!

Refreshing Scriptures

Gideons International is the oldest Christian business and professional men's organization in the United States. Founded in 1899, its purpose is to influence people for Christ by placing copies of the Bible in the traffic lanes of life. Right now, the Gideons are placing fifty-nine million Bibles a year in hotel rooms, hospitals, nursing homes, domestic-violence shelters, prisons, jails, and rescue missions all around the world. Obviously, their emphasis is on getting the Scriptures into the hands of hard-road travelers who need to be refreshed. And why not? Proverbs 18:4 says, "Words of true wisdom are as refreshing as a bubbling brook."

Joel would attest to that.

Several years ago, his wife of fourteen years discovered that he was having an affair and threw him out of their house. After checking into a motel, he picked up the phone and called the woman he'd been seeing on the sly for several months. Their time had come, he told her. They could finally end the charade. They could quit lying and sneaking around and bring their relationship out into the open once and for all. It wasn't happening exactly the way he'd planned, but maybe it was for the best. At least now they could get their divorces and finally be together all the time.

Except for one thing.

His "lover" suddenly wasn't so sure she was in love. At least not *that* much in love. Sure, they'd had some fun together and she liked him a lot. But, she explained, their pillow talk had gotten a little out of hand. She assumed it was all just part of the secret fantasy life they were living. She thought he understood that she never really intended to leave her husband.

As he hung up the phone, Joel felt despair like nothing he'd ever experienced. In one hour he'd gone from thinking he was the smoothest dude on the planet to feeling like a complete failure. And worse, a complete idiot. He'd actually thought the woman loved him. He'd believed all of her promises. He'd thrown his marriage away for her. How could he have been so stupid?

He sat at the motel room desk with his face in his hands, feeling the poisonous mixture of anger and humiliation burning in his chest. In front of him, not more than eighteen inches away, was a Gideon Bible. He stared at it for several seconds and felt the sudden urge to pick it up and start reading. But he quickly banished the thought. Instead, he decided to go out and drink himself into a stupor.

The next morning he awoke in a hospital bed. He didn't remember it, but they told him he'd driven his car into a tree. He had a broken leg, cracked ribs, a broken nose, and the first drunk-driving charge of his life. The car was a total loss. The doctor told him he was lucky to be alive.

It didn't take him long to spot the Gideon Bible sitting on the table beside his bed. It looked just like the one in the motel room. It was the same color and everything. He didn't reach for it at first. In fact, he tried to ignore it. But his eyes kept drifting to it as if it were a flashing neon light. Finally he picked it up.

He hadn't held a Bible in his hands in more than thirty years, but somehow it seemed familiar. Perhaps those countless childhood trips to Sunday school hadn't been wasted after all. He flipped from the front to the back, seeing the familiar book titles—names that hadn't crossed his mind in years—and finally settled on Isaiah. He didn't know why, really, except that he remembered his mother saying it was her favorite book.

No doubt it was God who directed his fingers as he turned the pages forward and back, finally ending up at Isaiah 55:6–7:

Seek the LORD while you can find him. Call on him now while he is near. Let the people turn from their wicked deeds. Let them banish from their minds the very thought of doing wrong! Let them turn to the LORD that he may have mercy on them. Yes, turn to our God, for he will abundantly pardon.

To this day, Joel points to that moment as the beginning of his turnaround. He will tell you that he was all but dead in his own personal wilderness of sin when he suddenly came across the oasis of God's Word. Yes, it took him a good while to get his life put back together and to repair the damage he'd caused, but he worked at it steadily and even managed to save his marriage.

My friend, how long has it been since you took a refreshing drink from the bubbling brook that is the Bible? Oddly enough, I know suffering people who have multiple copies of the Bible in their homes, yet never pick them up and read them. That would be like dying of thirst with four or five water spigots in your house!

Right now, a refreshing oasis could be as close as your nearest bookshelf. If you're feeling thirsty, why not take a drink? I promise, no matter how you wound up in the wilderness—whether it was your fault, someone else's fault, or nobody's fault—God has just the message you need to hear. Let me encourage you, before this day ends, to sit down with your Bible and pray the prayer of David in Psalm 119:25. He said, "I lie in the dust, completely discouraged; revive me by your word." And then, with an open heart and mind, start reading.

A Refreshing Savior

In my opinion, the most refreshing verse in the Bible is Matthew 11:28. Jesus said, "Come to me, all of you who are weary and carry heavy burdens, and I will give you rest." Let's think about this verse for a moment.

First, it's obvious that Jesus has a heart for hard-road travelers. No doubt that's because He was one. He, of all people, knows how it feels to be weary. And talk about burdens! Who ever carried a heavier one than He did?

Speaking of burdens, you should know that people in Bible times were experts when it came to transporting heavy objects. The great pyramids and even Solomon's temple were constructed without the use of heavy equipment. Even today, experts are baffled as to exactly how they managed to excavate gigantic blocks of stone and move them perfectly into place, one after another, with pure manpower.

But even with their engineering genius, they still buckled under the weight of religious persecution (John 15:20), financial hardship (Luke 21:2–3), marital problems (Matt. 5:27–32), parenting challenges (Luke 15:11–32), and health concerns (Mark 1:34). Isn't it interesting how millennia can pass, but some things never change? The hard roads of life are crowded in every generation.

Second, it's clear that Jesus doesn't discriminate when it comes to refreshing hard-road travelers. He says, "Come unto Me, *all of you* . . ." Okay, so maybe you aren't an important person in the world's eyes. Maybe you have very few friends. Maybe you're the kind of person people barely notice. Well, take heart. Jesus notices you and cares deeply about your welfare.

If you want proof, think about Jesus' attitude toward lepers. Leprosy is a horribly painful and disfiguring disease. It literally eats away at your extremities a little at a time. Fingers and toes and even noses can rot and fall off. Oozing sores are common. In those days, no group of people would have been more ostracized. Lepers were kept away from "respectable" society. For a healthy person to have contact of any kind with a leper would have been unthinkable.

But Jesus did.

In fact, in Luke 5:13 we're told that Jesus actually reached out and touched a leper when He healed him. Of course, He didn't have to touch him to heal him. He could have healed him from a distance as He did on other occasions (Luke 17:12–14). But Jesus apparently *wanted* to touch the man, and I can think of only one reason why. The touch was part of the refreshing. The man likely hadn't felt a gentle human touch in years. It was no doubt something he longed for, and Jesus wanted to fulfill that longing.

I love this about my Lord. In a world where status is so important, He is no respecter of persons. He loves everyone, even the hard-road travelers the masses have cast aside. Speaking of Jesus, Isaiah 42:7 says, "You will open the eyes of the blind and free the captives from prison. You will release those who sit in dark dungeons."

And finally, Jesus leaves no doubt about where hard-road travelers can go to find rest. He says, "Come unto *Me* and *I* will give you rest."

He doesn't say, "Go to your church."

Or "Go to your pastor."

Or "Go to your small group."

Or "Go to your therapist."

He says, "Come unto *Me*."

Keep in mind, I am a pastor. I have worked in churches for well over half my life. I know the tremendous blessings to be found in fellowship with other believers. But I will be the first to tell you that there is a kind of rest only Jesus can give. It's the "peace that passes understanding" you may have heard people talk about. To me, it's a deeply felt, all-encompassing sense of well-being that isn't affected by circumstances. It's joy that can't be shaken. And it's something I can't give, and neither can the church. It comes only from Jesus.

Right now on television, Gatorade commercials seem to be running about every ten minutes, especially during sports programming. They always show heavily perspiring athletes stretching themselves to the limits of endurance with drops of sweat rolling off them that are—*surprise!*—the color of Gatorade. And then comes the question: "Is it in you?"

I will agree that what's in you is important, but believe me, there's something more refreshing than Gatorade. Jesus said, "If you are thirsty, come to me! If you believe in me, come and drink!" (John 7:37–38).

Is *He* in you?

My friend, as bleak and desolate as the road ahead may look to you right now, there is reason for hope. God Himself said, "I will make springs in the desert, so that my chosen people can be refreshed" (Isa. 43:20). If you haven't found one of those springs yet, you will. Just keep going. It might be waiting for you over the next sand dune.

While Moses was at Kadesh, he sent ambassadors to the king of Edom with this message: "This message is from your relatives, the people of Israel: You know all the hardships we have been through, and that our ancestors went down to Egypt. We lived there a long time and suffered as slaves to the Egyptians. But when we cried out to the LORD, he heard us and sent an angel who brought us out of Egypt. Now we are camped at Kadesh, a town on the border of your land. Please let us pass through your country. We will be careful not to go through your fields and vineyards. We won't even drink water from your wells. We will stay on the king's road and never leave it until we have crossed the opposite border."

But the king of Edom said, "Stay out of my land or I will meet you with an army!"

The Israelites answered, "We will stay on the main road. If any of our livestock drinks your water, we will pay for it. We only want to pass through your country and nothing else."

But the king of Edom replied, "Stay out! You may not pass through our land." With that he mobilized his army and marched out to meet them with an imposing force. Because Edom refused to allow Israel to pass through their country, Israel was forced to turn around.

—NUMBERS 20:14–21

Expect Detours

He has twisted the road before me with many detours.

—LAMENTATIONS 3:9

It wasn't an unreasonable request.

All the Israelites wanted to do was cut through the land of Edom on their way to Canaan. It was the most direct route and would have saved them a lot of time and energy. Moses, a respectful man who understood the importance of protocol, sent his representatives to place a request for safe passage and to assure the king of Edom that nothing in his country would be disturbed. Moses promised that they would stay on the main road and refrain from drinking water from the many wells that dotted the countryside. He even reminded the king that they were kin, since both nations descended from Abraham and Isaac. Surely, Moses thought, this one small favor wasn't too much to ask.

But the king of Edom disagreed.

In a striking show of belligerence, he rallied his troops to the border and said, in essence, "If you set one foot on our land, you'll be sorry!" Of course, Moses could have consulted God on the matter. It's possible that God would have said, "Go ahead and pass through the land of Edom. And don't worry about that old king. I'll show him who's boss!" But Moses chose not to take the problem to God. He seemed to understand that detours are a normal part of life.

And so they are.

Our entire nation was reminded of this when it was announced that many of our soldiers in Iraq would be staying longer than was originally planned. One young woman I know was counting the days (and probably the hours and minutes) until she would be able to return to the States and see her husband and two children. As a family, they were firing e-mails back and forth on a daily basis, excitedly making plans for her homecoming, which was less than three weeks away. But then came the announcement that her unit's tour of duty was being extended for several months. The news hit the entire family like a blow to the stomach.

Life is full of surprises, and not all of them are pleasant. You can be cruising right along toward your desired destination and even be ahead of schedule when, suddenly, a Road Closed or a Bridge Out sign pops up in front of you and sends you off in a completely different direction. Few experiences are more disheartening, especially when you're already growing weary. Just the thought of a longer road with even more challenges can break your spirit.

That's why I want to spend the rest of this chapter helping you prepare for the detours you will likely face on your hard road home. There are four facts you need to understand.

A Detour Can Trick You

It can mess with your mind. It can have you believing that God has abandoned you or, worse yet, that He has turned against you for some reason. But a detour doesn't necessarily mean any such thing. In fact, many detours have turned out to be real blessings.

Not long ago I read about the Clarks, a family of eleven, who lived in Great Britain almost a hundred years ago. They believed a better life could be found in America, so they scrimped and saved for years until they had enough money to secure passports and buy tickets for the transatlantic voyage. But just a week before they were supposed to leave, the youngest son was bitten by a dog. The doctor treated the wound, but the possibility of rabies required the entire family to be quarantined for fourteen days.

Just that quickly, the family's dream was snuffed out. They'd wasted their money on tickets they couldn't use and would have to start saving all over again from scratch. Mr. Clark was beside himself and angrily cursed God for being so heartless. But he changed his tune just five days later when he heard that the ship they were supposed to be sailing on had sunk.[1]

More recently, a young woman stumbled and fell down a flight of stairs, breaking her ankle, just a few weeks before her wedding. Immediately she postponed the ceremony. She didn't care that it was a major hassle to reschedule everything. She simply refused to come hobbling down the aisle on crutches.

Naturally, she was frustrated, not to mention angry at herself for not watching her step. How could she, a former gymnast, have been so thoughtless and clumsy? How is it that she could do all sorts of difficult somersaults and backflips in competition, and then suddenly demonstrate all the grace of an elephant on roller skates while merely walking down a flight of stairs? She viewed the accident as an ugly intrusion on her fairy-tale life and was more than a little irritated at God for not doing a better job of watching over her.

But if you were to talk to that young woman today, she would tell you that her detour turned out to be a blessing. You see, it was during her recovery period that her fiancé was arrested for trying to sell illegal drugs to an undercover cop. She'd had no idea the man she was about to marry was involved in criminal activity. Immediately, she called off the wedding, ended the relationship, and praised God for sparing her what would have been a disastrous marriage.

Isn't it interesting how quickly we can go from blaming God to praising Him? One little fact—one little nugget of truth suddenly revealed—is all it takes to completely transform our feelings and show us how wrong we were to assume the worst. What I can't figure out is why we don't just go ahead and assume the *best* in every situation from the get-go. Even if we can't actually see the good at first, why not just go ahead and believe it's there? After all, God said, "I know the plans I have for you . . . They are plans for good and not for disaster, to give you a future and a hope" (Jer. 29:11). And Romans 8:28 says, "God causes everything to work together for the good of those who love God and are called according to his purpose for them." Either we believe those words or we don't. If we do, then we must believe that God is always working—and even using detours—to unfold His *positive* plan for our lives.

A great example in Scripture would be the apostle Paul.

Called to be the apostle to the Gentiles, he had mountains of work to do for the Lord. Far too much to spend time sitting in a prison cell. Yet, circumstances parked him there a number of times—once for about five years! I'm sure he must have been incredibly frustrated when those shackles were first clamped around his wrists. But that sixty-month detour turned out to be one of the most productive periods of his life, for it was while he was behind bars that he was given the opportunity to share his testimony with some of the most powerful political leaders on earth (Acts 24–25). While in prison he also led countless people to Christ, including Onesimus (Philem. 10), and even found the time to write five books of the Bible. One of those, Philippians, is the favorite of many hard-road travelers because of its unwavering optimism.

The next time you encounter a detour, don't be tricked. It may appear on the surface to be the worst thing that could have happened. But if you're willing to reserve judgment and be patient, you might see it turn out to be the best. Don't forget Proverbs 16:9: "We can make our plans, but the LORD determines our steps." He is still calling the shots, even when it seems as though circumstances are taking us off course.

A Detour Can Teach You

Do you believe in love at first sight?

There's a part of me that wants to say it's all just a hoax that songwriters and greeting card companies have concocted to make money. I mean, honestly, can a woman really fall in love with someone the second her eyes fall on him? It just seems to me like the stuff fairy tales are made of. And yet, every time I read the story of Jacob and Rachel in Genesis 29, I'm forced to admit that it really does happen occasionally.

You may recall how Jacob was standing beside a well, asking some shepherds for directions to his uncle Laban's estate, when Laban's daughter Rachel approached with a small flock of sheep. Rachel must have been a real looker, because poor Jacob took one look at her and was almost knocked off his feet. If there had been a movie sound track playing in the background at that moment, you can bet the violins would have hit a rapturous crescendo. Suddenly, Jacob wanted to do something—*anything*—to make an impression on her (a typical guy!), so he single-handedly moved a huge stone that was covering the mouth of the well. Knowing how guys are, I suspect he even positioned himself so she could see his bulging biceps. And then, with a spring in his step, he watered her flocks.

What happened next is right out of an afternoon soap opera or a

Harlequin romance. Genesis 29:11 says, "Then Jacob kissed Rachel, and tears came to his eyes." I see only two possible explanations for the tears. Either the passion of the moment touched the very depths of his soul, or she had really bad breath. I'm pretty sure it was the passion he felt that made him weep.

Naturally, the next order of business was to make this gorgeous woman his wife. The problem was that her father, Laban, whom Jacob barely knew, was a con man. He was sneaky and conniving, the master of the shady deal. After making him work a month without pay (isn't it amazing what a lovesick young man will do?), Laban finally asked Jacob what he'd like his wages to be. The poor guy must have blurted his answer without thinking. He said, "I'll work for you seven years if you'll give me Rachel, your younger daughter, as my wife" (Gen. 29:18). Why he didn't choose a shorter period of time, I haven't a clue. I know I would have. But the deal was struck and the clock started ticking.

And then comes the most romantic verse in the Bible. I mean, this is real swoon material. Verse 20 says, "So Jacob spent the next seven years working to pay for Rachel. But his love for her was so strong that it seemed to him but a few days."

Wow.

That's the stuff operas and sonnets and Hallmark cards are made of. The two of them definitely appear to be on a collision course with a fairy-tale ending. I can just see Jacob clocking out on his 2,555th day of work, splashing on a little cologne, and heading straight to the wedding feast. After all, they had seven years to plan the wedding, and I'm confident he was in no mood to waste any more time.

But something went terribly wrong.

When Jacob woke up the next morning, he found that he had made love to Rachel's homely older sister, Leah! Laban, the schemer, had slipped her into Jacob's bed in the dark, and Jacob, who may have been a little tipsy after all the partying, didn't notice. Can you imagine the horror you would feel if you opened your eyes on the morning after your wedding night and realized you were cuddling the wrong person?

Talk about a detour on the way to bliss!

The Bible says Jacob "raged" at Laban (29:25), who quickly offered an explanation. "It's not our custom to marry off a younger daughter ahead of the firstborn," he said, I suspect, with a smirk (v. 26). And then, just to show that he wasn't a bad guy after all, he proposed a solution. (No doubt he'd had it in mind all along.) He said that if Jacob could just wait until the end of the marriage week of celebration, he could have Rachel, too, in return for seven more years of labor (v. 27). So what was Jacob going to say? "No thanks, I'll just forget about my soul mate and raise a family with this homely girl that I don't even love"? Of course not! He took the only option that was going to make Rachel his wife. But it was a choice that would also bring endless headaches into his life. The Bible tells us that resentment and jealousy raged between the two sisters, catching Jacob squarely in the middle. Before long their home became a boiling cauldron of sexual and emotional tension.

In case you're wondering if Jacob and Rachel ever found happiness, they did. Even with all the hardships, theirs was truly a love for the ages. But it wasn't the straight shot to bliss that they were expecting. They were forced to take some bumpy side roads that served as a sort of "school of hard knocks." Among the lessons Jacob learned in that fabled university were:

- *don't make deals with people you don't really know;*

- *read the fine print;*

- *check the ID of every person who crawls into your bed.*

Yes indeed, a detour can teach you.

So if the road you're following is ever blocked by a Road Closed sign, don't panic. Just figure you're about to learn a lesson or two. They may or may not be as painful as the lessons Jacob learned, but they will likely be just as valuable. So pay close attention.

A Detour Can Train You

The difference between teaching and training is the difference between knowledge and experience. Sometimes, like Jacob, we simply need to learn some lessons. Other times, like David, we need to learn some skills.

You may recall that David was anointed by Samuel to be the king of Israel in 1 Samuel 16 but was not allowed to assume the throne immediately because King Saul already occupied it. David was young and needed some seasoning, but Saul knew his time was coming, so he decided to be proactive and remove him from the picture. And by remove him, I mean kill him. David literally had to "head for the hills" in order to survive. For years, he lived as a fugitive, creeping through the countryside, hiding out in caves, and experiencing one close call after another.

But that unpleasant detour enabled him to gain some valuable experience, as the following verses indicate:

> David left Gath and escaped to the cave of Adullam. Soon his brothers and other relatives joined him there. Then others began coming—men who were in trouble or in debt or who were just discontented—until David was the leader of about four hundred men. (1 Sam. 22:1–2)

David quickly turned that group of shirttail relatives, crooks, deadbeats, and malcontents into a fierce fighting machine and led them victoriously into one battle after another. Clearly, his fugitive days, as unpleasant as they may have been, gave him an opportunity to develop the leadership skills and military know-how he would need when he finally did assume the throne.

However—and this is important!—David didn't see it this way at the time. He never said, "Boy, I sure am glad these hardships have come into my life! I just know I'll be a better king because I've had to live in a cave and sleep on the cold, hard ground!" In fact, there were times when David didn't think he was going to survive long enough to even be king (1 Sam. 27:1). But whether he realized the benefits of his detour or not, God was steadily working through those difficult circumstances to prepare him for the most important work of his life.

Have you considered the possibility that God has some great task or ministry that He wants you to perform? And that by stretching out your hard-road journey He's actually preparing you for it?

A Detour Will Test You

Douglas "Pete" Peterson became the first U.S. ambassador to Vietnam in 1997. What made his appointment headline news is the fact that he, like John McCain, spent almost seven years in Vietnam as a prisoner of war. He was captured shortly after being shot down on a bombing mission near Hanoi in 1966.

Pete Peterson's nightmarish detour tested his will to live, his courage, his faith, his resourcefulness, and his endurance. But what it may have tested more than anything else was his character. You see, when he was finally released, he, like all the other

POWs, had to decide how he was going to process and deal with what had happened. Many of the POWs became bitter, and no one would have blamed him if he'd done the same. I know I couldn't guarantee that I wouldn't be filled with resentment if somebody stole six and a half years of my life. But Pete Peterson handled the experience with extraordinary grace. He proved the strength of his character when, in the course of his duties as ambassador, he was required to work with the very people who had imprisoned him and treated them with respect and professional courtesy.

Pete Peterson's story reminds me of Joseph in Scripture, who also had some of his youth stolen. He was sold into slavery by his older brothers at the age of seventeen. Thirteen years later, God placed him in a position of great authority in Egypt. He controlled the nation's food supplies and could easily have used his position to seek retribution against his brothers, who came to him for help during a time of famine. But he, like Pete Peterson, understood that holding a grudge serves no positive purpose. Sticking it to his brothers wasn't going to give him back those lost days. So he chose, instead, to forgive them and move on with his life.

A detour will always test your character, because it so naturally breeds anger and frustration. It gives you a perfect opportunity to throw a screaming fit without anybody really blaming you. But it also gives you an opportunity to put forth an exceptional witness. If you can trust God and remain faithful even on the difficult side roads of life, you will impact a lot of people.

I once had a church member who'd endured seventeen major surgeries. That's seventeen detours from the road she would have preferred to follow. That she could even walk upright after all she'd been through was amazing to me. I'll never forget the day I asked her how she managed to keep such a positive attitude. She said, "I see every one of my surgeries as a pulpit from which I get to proclaim the awesome power of God."

She passed her test with flying colors.

I hope you do too.

I'm sure you remember *Gilligan's Island*, the goofy 1960s sitcom about a group of people stranded on a deserted island. I will confess that few shows in the history of television have annoyed me as much as that one did. When the skipper took off his hat and started whopping Gilligan over the head with it, I wanted to join in. Anybody that idiotic deserves to be whopped. If it hadn't been for Ginger and Mary Ann, the show would have had no redeeming value whatsoever!

But as much as I hated the program, I will admit that it inspired me to coin a term I have used in many counseling sessions over the years. I often refer to the Gilligan's Island Factor when talking about how life sometimes sends us places we never intended to go. Remember, the SS *Minnow* embarked on what was supposed to be a three-hour tour, but the weather started getting rough, the tiny ship was tossed, and, well, you know the song. Without warning, the vacationers found themselves on a serious detour.

But I will give the castaways credit for one thing: They sure made the most of their situation. They lived in comfortable quarters, ate gourmet meals, and always wore clothing that looked as if it just came back from the cleaners. And with the professor's help, they were able to rig up just about every appliance imaginable with cane poles, palm fronds, and a little twine. (Didn't you ever wonder how they could build what amounted to a small village and equip it with all sorts of modern conveniences, but couldn't fix a hole in the side of their boat?)

Gilligan's Island may have been a goofy show about imaginary people, but trust me: The Gilligan's Island Factor is as real as the book you're holding in your hands. Almost everybody is blown off course sooner or later. Three-hour tours can become four-year detours before you know it.

If it happens to you, don't panic. Believe that God still loves you and is still in control. Make up your mind that you're willing to learn whatever the experience is ready to teach you. And remember that your character is being put to the test. People are watching and will be influenced for better or worse by what you say and do.

The LORD said to Moses, "Give the Israelites instructions regarding the LORD's appointed festivals, the days when all of you will be summoned to worship me. You may work for six days each week, but on the seventh day all work must come to a complete stop. It is the LORD's Sabbath day of complete rest, a holy day to assemble for worship. It must be observed wherever you live."

—LEVITICUS 23:1–3

Worship on the Way

*You must fear the L*ORD *your God*
and worship him and cling to him.
—DEUTERONOMY 10:20

Yesterday was Mother's Day and, as always, I preached a Mother's Day sermon. But it wasn't easy. As I stood in the pulpit and looked out over the congregation, I saw quite a number of sad faces. One of them belonged to a twenty-three-year-old college senior whose mother committed suicide. Another belonged to a kindhearted woman whose son was recently arrested for the third time. A few belonged to single moms who were struggling to make ends meet. And several more belonged to women whose unbelieving husbands were home in bed, on the golf course, or down at the fishing hole.

As I preached, I felt a deep sense of admiration for these hard-road travelers who knew full well that worship on this day would bring some heartache, but decided to show up anyway. They obviously understood what I am going to try to express in this chapter, that worship is especially important for those on the hard roads of life.

I find it interesting that as the Israelites embarked on their hard-road journey, God took great pains to ensure that worship would

127

hold a prominent place in their lives. In Exodus 25:8, He said, "I want the people of Israel to build me a sacred residence where I can live among them." Both Abraham and Moses (and Aaron, if you remember the golden calf episode) had built altars in various places, but God wanted them to build Him a permanent yet portable dwelling that would also provide a place for Him to meet with the people (Ex. 25:22). So the tabernacle, which means "tent of meeting," was built and furnished according to God's exact specifications. Several items, including the ark of the covenant, were kept inside to serve as constant reminders of God's goodness and faithfulness, and detailed worship procedures were instituted by God so the people would understand how and when to come before Him.

Of course, the tabernacle was only the beginning. Solomon later built the temple, which was patterned after the tabernacle, and today modern houses of worship can be found in almost every community. History shows that God's people have indeed understood the value of corporate worship and dedicated themselves to it. And in recent years, worship has moved even more toward the center of things. Many wonderful worship leaders and an abundance of resources have helped invigorate churches all across the country. I'm even noticing a refreshing evolution in terminology these days. Instead of just "going to church," I'm hearing more and more Christians talking about "going to worship."

But even with these positive developments, worship can still be pretty tough for the hard-road traveler. Recently, a woman whose husband abandoned her walked out of our auditorium while I was preaching about marriage. Later, she said, "Your sermon was wonderful. It really was. But I was sitting there all alone for the first time in my life, and I couldn't quit thinking about my husband and his new girlfriend. I tried not to think about them, but I was getting all sorts of images flashing through my mind. I just had to get out of there before I came unglued."

Have you had a similar experience?

Has your hard road made worship painful?

Maybe it's painful for you to listen to your preacher talk about how God answers prayer, when you've been praying hard about your devastating situation for months (or even years) and are still waiting for your first answer.

Maybe it's painful for you to sing songs about the riches of God's blessings when you're working two jobs and still can't stay caught up on your bills.

Or maybe you're like the woman who once said to me, "It's just hard to be around so many perky, upbeat people when you feel like a piece of garbage."

Yes, for the hard-road traveler, corporate worship can be tough. Satan will always be there to plant negative thoughts in your mind. He'll suggest that what you're getting out of worship isn't worth the heartache you're having to endure. He'll assure you that all of those giddy, happy-faced people around you don't give a rip about you and your problems. He'll try to convince you that a little break from "the church thing" would do you good, at least until your situation turns around. And for good measure, he'll remind you that there are preachers on TV if you ever feel you need a little dose of religion.

But you can't buy into his lies if you hope to survive your ordeal. There are at least four reasons why you simply must continue to worship.

Worship Nourishes Your Relationship with God

I shudder to think what might have happened to the Israelites during their forty-year trek through the wilderness if God hadn't insisted that they make worship a priority. Even with the tabernacle and its reminders of God's goodness and faithfulness, the people often wavered in their faith and disobeyed Him. Without those things, they surely would have abandoned Him altogether.

I say "surely" because, if there's one thing I've learned in all my years as a pastor, it's that God's people must worship regularly in order to keep their faith alive. And again, I'm not talking about listening to a Christian CD in your car as you're driving to work or praising God for His beautiful creation when you pull an eight-pound bass out of your local fishing hole, though there's obviously nothing wrong with those things. I'm talking about corporate worship—gathering with other believers on a regular basis to pray, sing praises, and listen to the preached Word. Yes, I've heard all the arguments from the I-can-be-a-Christian-without-going-to-church crowd, but I've never seen any evidence that their claims are true. In my experience, every time a Christian drops out of church and abandons corporate worship, he starts sinking spiritually. Maybe not the first day or the first week, but eventually. I can't recall a single exception.

And if the average Christian sinks, you can just imagine what happens to those hard-road travelers who have the ball and chain of adversity clamped to their ankles. I've seen them disappear beneath the murky waters of despair almost instantly. They let go of the one thing that's helping them stay afloat and, suddenly, they're gone.

That's why the Bible insists that believers meet together for worship. Hebrews 10:25 says, "Let us not neglect our meeting together, as some people do, but *encourage and warn each other*, especially now that the day of his coming back again is drawing near" (emphasis added). I don't know a single preacher who isn't in love with that verse. We quote those first ten words until our jaws are sore in an effort to pump up church attendance. But I'm afraid we haven't given enough attention to the middle of the verse. If we are to keep our faith alive, we need to be *encouraged* and *warned* when we come together. That means some real heart-level stuff needs to be happening in our worship services. I love air-conditioning, padded pews, contemporary music, drama skits, and movie clips as much as the next guy. But those things mean little if they're not reaching deep into the hearts of people. It's easy for church leaders to become obsessed with putting together a dazzling worship service that sends people out the door raving about how talented our singers and musicians are and to pat ourselves on the back when we reach that goal. But the bigger question is, are we encouraging and warning our people? The moment we stop doing that, the sinking will begin in earnest, no matter how flashy our worship services are.

With that thought in mind, I'd like to offer a word of advice to those who may be looking for a place to worship. Maybe you've recently moved to a new community or, for some other reason, are currently without a church home. Let me urge you to look for a place to worship that will both encourage and warn you. Most churches will at least attempt to do the former, but a lot of them will purposely avoid the latter. Why? Because warnings are generally negative in tone, and many congregations, in their blind desire to be seeker-friendly, are scared to death to say anything negative for fear they might make a poor impression on a prospect.

Call me old-fashioned, but I long for a day when boldness returns to our pulpits. As I read the Scriptures, I can't find a single prophet of God who ever minced words. In fact, they continually got themselves into deep trouble by being so blunt. Even Jesus at times causes us to cringe with His incisive comments. Yet, in churches far and wide, there is a concerted effort to tone down the gospel, to steer clear of its more controversial elements and make it more palatable.

Could this be why so many professing believers are living such worldly, messed-up lives? A Christian counselor I know told me recently that she's never seen such a flood of confused and dysfunctional Christians coming through her doors.

As a longtime member of the preaching fraternity, it's hard for me to say this, but I just can't shake the feeling that too many of us have gone soft. I'm afraid we're making people happy, but not holy. I'm afraid we're wooing them, but not warning them.

Let me encourage you to continue your search for a church home until you find one that offers the whole counsel of God. Don't stop looking until you find a preacher who's courageous enough to step on your toes now and then. When I was a very young preacher, an elderly gentleman said to me, "Mark, if you don't poke me at least once in every sermon, you're not doing your job." That's debatable, of course. But you get the idea. Your relationship with God will wither without worship.

Worship Guarantees Your Protection

I'm guessing that you don't spend a lot of your Bible reading time in the book of Ezra. It's one of those books that even devout Christians have to turn to the table of contents to find. But it's a great story, and one scene in particular speaks clearly to the subject at hand.

Here's a little background.

The Babylonian army destroyed Jerusalem around 587 BC, and the people of Judah were taken into exile. About fifty years later, the Babylonian Empire was overthrown by the Persians, and the new ruler, Cyrus, actually encouraged the exiles to return to their homeland and rebuild. As you might expect, some of the Jews had become so comfortable that they chose not to return. But many did, and the first six chapters of Ezra tell the story of how that first wave of about fifty thousand Jews struggled to rebuild the temple in Jerusalem. They finally completed it in about 515.

Then, starting in chapter 7, we read about another group of returnees, led by Ezra. He was a scholar and a man of great faith who made the journey with about two thousand of his countrymen, many of whom were priests. His purpose is explicitly stated in the text: "Ezra had determined to study and obey the law of the LORD and to teach those laws and regulations to the people of Israel" (7:10). Simply put, his goal was to teach the people how to worship properly in their new temple.

It's Ezra's journey back to Jerusalem that I want to highlight.

It was going to take about five months and would be very dangerous. The people were not seasoned fighters and had few weapons, making them an inviting target for bands of outlaws and rogue armies. Ezra considered asking the king for a military escort, but then decided against it because of a statement he'd already made to the king. He'd said, "Our God protects all those who worship him, but his fierce anger rages against those who abandon him" (8:22). If he really believed that and wanted the king to believe it also, how could he then act as if he didn't believe it? Wouldn't that destroy his testimony? In Ezra's mind, the answer was yes. So he and his followers made the trip without an armed escort. They worshipped on the way, fasting and praying earnestly for God's protection, which He graciously provided.

But let's go back to the statement Ezra made to the king.

He said, "Our God protects all those who worship him, but his fierce anger rages against those who abandon him."

The thing that is so striking (and frightening) about this verse is that it pictures two extremes and nothing in the middle. It seems to suggest that you either worship God or abandon Him. I know we'd like to believe there are more choices than that. We'd like to think there's some sort of middle ground where we could still be in fellowship with God without actually making worship a priority. I see people attempt this all the time. They drop out of church, completely remove corporate worship from their lives, and then tell themselves they're okay because they still love Jesus.

But look at the statement again: "Our God protects all those who worship him, but his fierce anger rages against those who abandon him."

Where, exactly, is the middle ground? It looks to me as if you either worship God and enjoy His protection, or you abandon Him and forfeit His protection. And everything I see around me confirms that.

Just yesterday I spoke to a woman who used to attend our church with her family. While they were here, they made good progress in their faith and saw their family relationships, which had been severely strained, healed. But then a comment was made by another church member that the woman found offensive, prompting her to pull her family out of church. I spoke to her at the time and literally pleaded with her to forgive the individual, but she seemed determined to make as big an issue as she could out of her injury.

Well, I ran into her yesterday, and we struck up a conversation. And sure enough, her family has fallen on hard times. Over the last few months, layoffs, financial problems, and some health problems have battered them and created real tension in the home. In fact, she had bags under her eyes that I'd never seen before and looked very unkempt, which was unusual. As delicately as possible, I tried to remind her that they enjoyed their best days while they were in church, but she immediately started talking about the woman who'd spoken the unkind words. She seemed obsessed with the incident even after several months. And what's worse, she seemed blind to what she and her family had lost.

"Our God protects all those who worship him, but his fierce anger rages against those who abandon him."

My friend, please underline or highlight Ezra's statement in your Bible. In fact, if you're a person who has a hard time getting to church on a regular basis, it might even be a good idea for you to print a few copies and stick them in places where you'll see the verse often and be reminded of the risk you're taking. You're already on a hard road, a road that produces many casualties (see Chapter 4). You simply cannot afford to forfeit God's protection.

Worship Improves Your Outlook

Have you ever been to a sporting event and heard a cheer go up for no apparent reason? If you go to a Cardinals game in St. Louis on a Sunday afternoon in September, you're liable to hear the crowd roar its approval even when the Redbirds are getting spanked. Why? Because the St. Louis Rams will be playing football at the same time and the people at the baseball game who are also football fans will have their transistor radios tuned in. When the Rams score a touchdown, a hearty cheer will go up, even if a Cardinal player has just struck out.

In life, there's always more going on than what you can see in front of you. Even when your circumstances grow very difficult, there are still reasons to rejoice. The trick is to stay "tuned in" to those reasons, which is where worship comes in. Nothing reminds you that you have a lot to be thankful for like a powerful encounter with God. In Scripture, Elijah is one person who made this discovery.

In 1 Kings 18, he had a confrontation with 450 prophets of the false god Baal, and ended up slaughtering every one of them. Because Baal worship had stolen the people's hearts away from the one true God, that horrifying bloodbath was considered a great victory and was, arguably, the high point of Elijah's life of service to God. But it also inflamed his Baal-worshipping enemies. Jezebel, in particular, the evil queen of Israel who was responsible for introducing Baal worship to the people, was furious. In a fit of rage, she swore to have Elijah killed within twenty-four hours and immediately dispatched a team of hit men to track him down. When he heard the news, his faith immediately melted away and he sank into a deep depression. Things suddenly looked so hopeless that he saw no point in carrying on with his life (1 Kings 19:4).

The conversation he had with God at that point is particularly telling. He said, "I have zealously served the LORD God Almighty. But the people of Israel have broken their covenant with you, torn down your altars, and killed every one of your prophets. I alone am left, and now they are trying to kill me, too" (1 Kings 19:10). From Elijah's perspective, everything looked dismal. There wasn't a single reason to have hope. But again, there's always more going on than what you can see in front of you. After giving Elijah a few amazing demonstrations of His power, God gave His discouraged servant some good news. He told him that, no, he wasn't the only believer left. There were still seven thousand Israelites who had not bowed down to Baal (1 Kings 19:18).

My friend, if your outlook on life has turned sour—if you're depressed by the turns your hard road has taken and have all but given up hope—you're exactly where Elijah was and you need just what he needed: some demonstrations of God's power and some good news. And where better to find those things than in a place where God's people meet for worship? The Bible says that when Christians meet together in His name, He is there! (Matt. 18:20). And one of the reasons He is there is to bless and encourage His children.

I will tell you right now that if you go with the right spirit to the right church, and open your heart to God, you *will* come away with a brighter outlook on life. I don't care how bleak and dismal your world looks when you walk in, worship just has a way of infusing our hearts with hope. I've seen it a thousand times. People walk into church frowning and walk out smiling. I've had countless people hug me with tears in their eyes and tell me the service meant more to them than they could even begin to express. It isn't me or our musicians who accomplish this; it's God, working through the power of His Spirit to minister to the needs of those who have come with open hearts into His presence.

Worship Enhances Your Witness

In one sense, we Christians shouldn't worry much about how we are perceived by others. We should accept that the world is always going to think much of what we do is foolishness. We are, after all, called to be a "peculiar people" (1 Peter 2:9 KJV).

But there is another sense in which we should be very concerned about how we are perceived. When it comes to our witness, our ability to reflect the character of Christ in our everyday lives, we simply can't be too careful.

Remember Abu Ghraib?

That was the name of the U.S. military prison in Iraq where a handful of American soldiers decided to have a little sick fun at the expense of some captured Iraqis. You remember the photos. Naked Iraqis were piled on top of one another, led around by leashes, and forced to simulate sex acts, all to the clicking accompaniment of a digital camera. We knew from day one that less than a dozen soldiers out of more than 140,000 disgraced their uniforms, but the entire military suffered a terrible black eye. Even the top decision makers who were half a world away when the crimes occurred had to scramble to save their jobs.

Do you realize you're wearing a uniform too? Paul said, "For all of you who were baptized into Christ have clothed yourselves with Christ" (Gal. 3:27 NIV). That's right, Jesus Himself is your uniform! When you accepted Him, you chose to wear His name and wrap yourself in His commands and promises. So anything you do (or don't do) that fails to meet His standards reflects poorly, not only on you, but also on Him.

The reason the power of your witness is so dependent on your commitment to corporate worship is because that's one of the most visible aspects of your Christian life. For the most part, your church friends don't see you during the week. They don't know what you do in the privacy of your home. But when you come walking into church, they know immediately that in spite of the difficulties you're facing, you haven't turned your back on the Lord.

Several years ago, a lady in our church was dying of cancer. She told me when she was first diagnosed that as long as she could put one foot in front of the other, she would be at church. And she was true to her word. I remember one day near the end of her life, she walked in looking thin and frail, taking little baby steps. Her skin was a sickly yellow color, her hair was almost gone, and her husband walked beside her, carrying an oxygen canister. He gently lowered her into a seat on the back row, and there she worshipped. A tear came to my eye when, during one of our praise songs that talks about lifting holy hands to the Lord, she lifted her skinny hands a few inches into the air. They trembled in weakness, but she held them there and, with her eyes closed and a little smile on her face, mouthed the words to the song.

There were two sermons preached in our church that day. I stood behind the pulpit and preached one, and she sat on the back row and preached another without saying a word. And I will tell you now that hers was the more powerful of the two.

My suffering friend, do you even begin to recognize the opportunity you have to inspire and encourage others? The very fact that life has dealt you a difficult blow means people will watch you closely. Secretly, they'll imagine themselves in your shoes. They'll wonder how they would react if the same thing happened to them. And if they see you maintaining your commitment to the Lord and continuing to build your faith in spite of your pain, they'll remember it later when they find themselves in a similar situation.

Even though it's now been several years since the lady I just mentioned died from her cancer, I can still close my eyes and see her as plain as day. And even though I knew her when she was perfectly healthy, that's not the image I see in my mind. I see her thin and frail, with yellowed skin and thinning hair. I see her with trembling hands reaching up toward the God she knew she was going to meet face-to-face very soon. And I see that smile—that sweet little smile that was obviously a reflection of the joy in her heart.

Just think.

I, and everyone else at church that Sunday, would have been robbed of an incredibly inspirational memory if she'd chosen to stay home. No one in his right mind would have blamed her. But if she had, today we'd all be just a little poorer.

Worship enhances your witness.

Two days ago, I did something I hate to do. I visited one of our church members at a cancer hospital in Tampa. Cancer hospitals have always been difficult for me because they are so bleak. No matter how hard the employees try to cheer them up (and God bless them for trying!), the suffering for both the patients and the families always seems to be cranked up a few notches from regular hospitals. When I arrived, the person I went to see was in a consultation with her doctor, so I took a seat in a small waiting area just down the hall. I was only there a few minutes, but something happened in that brief span of time that I know I'll always remember.

A woman walked in talking on a cell phone. She was dressed in a robe and slippers, and had the telltale yellow skin and a bandanna tied around her head to hide what I figured was a bald head. She looked bad, but if I had been blind I wouldn't have been able to tell by the sound of her voice that she was even sick. She sounded incredibly cheerful and laughed more than I would have thought possible for someone in her situation.

And then she spoke some words into her cell phone that I'll never forget: "Sweetheart, remember. My body is the only thing that's dying."

Was she talking to her husband? Or perhaps one of her children? I didn't know, but it was obvious she was telling the truth. Her body was dying, and quickly, it appeared. But you could tell from her words and the lilt in her voice that her spirit was soaring. Suddenly I remembered Paul's statement in 2 Corinthians 4:16: "Though our bodies are dying, our spirits are being renewed every day."

That's really the goal, isn't it?

Whatever happens and no matter how bad it gets, the goal is to keep our spirits alive and well. The only way I know of to do that is to keep worshipping.

A delegation from the tribe of Judah, led by Caleb son of Jephunneh the Kenizzite, came to Joshua at Gilgal. Caleb said to Joshua, "Remember what the LORD said to Moses, the man of God, about you and me when we were at Kadesh-barnea. I was forty years old when Moses, the servant of the LORD, sent me from Kadesh-barnea to explore the land of Canaan. I returned and gave from my heart a good report, but my brothers who went with me frightened the people and discouraged them from entering the Promised Land. For my part, I followed the LORD my God completely. So that day Moses promised me, 'The land of Canaan on which you were just walking will be your special possession and that of your descendants forever, because you wholeheartedly followed the LORD my God.'

"Now, as you can see, the LORD has kept me alive and well as he promised for all these forty-five years since Moses made this promise—even while Israel wandered in the wilderness. Today I am eighty-five years old. I am as strong now as I was when Moses sent me on that journey, and I can still travel and fight as well as I could then. So I'm asking you to give me the hill country that the LORD promised me. You will remember that as scouts we found the Anakites living there in great, walled cities. But if the LORD is with me, I will drive them out of the land, just as the LORD said."

So Joshua blessed Caleb son of Jephunneh and gave Hebron to him as an inheritance. Hebron still belongs to the descendants of Caleb son of Jephunneh the Kenizzite because he wholeheartedly followed the LORD, the God of Israel.

—JOSHUA 14:6–14

Keep Your Dreams Alive

Take delight in the LORD,
and he will give you your heart's desires.

—PSALM 37:4

Caleb was one of the original twelve spies that Moses sent to spy out the land of Canaan. During that forty-day period, I doubt he had anything on his mind other than fulfilling his mission and making it back to headquarters in one piece. I'm sure that finding his lifelong dream was the furthest thing from his mind. But when the team made its way deep into enemy territory and his eyes fell on the hill country of Hebron, his breath caught in his throat and a shiver ran down his spine. He'd never seen anything so beautiful and instantly knew he'd never have peace until he made that section of the Promised Land his home.

But a terrible thing happened on the way to his dream come true.

Ten of the twelve men on that reconnaissance team couldn't quit harping on the fact that the land was inhabited by a race of giants. To get the picture, imagine thousands of armor-plated, spear-toting warriors about twelve inches taller than Shaquille O'Neal. That would be enough to make anybody break out in a cold sweat! But

Caleb and Joshua pleaded with the people not to forget who was on *their* side. They begged their countrymen to place their trust in the God of miracles, who had just delivered them from the entire Egyptian army. They said, "Do not rebel against the LORD, and don't be afraid of the people of the land. They are only helpless prey to us! They have no protection, but the LORD is with us! Don't be afraid of them!" (Num. 14:9). But in the end, their begging and pleading fell on deaf ears. The fearmongers had whipped the people into such a state of panic that they refused to take even one step toward the land the Lord had promised to give them. This, as we have already seen, infuriated God and compelled Him to send them on a forty-year trek through the wilderness.

Poor Caleb.

The guy did absolutely nothing wrong, yet he had no choice but to put his dream on hold and go stomping off into the middle of nowhere with his cowardly countrymen. He'd been close enough to see his dream and even smell and taste it because the team had brought back samples of the enormous fruits and vegetables the fertile land was producing. But suddenly, with the pronouncement of God's punishment on his whining kinfolk, his dream must have seemed a million miles away. He probably felt as if it had been held out to him and then rudely snatched away before he could close his fingers around it.

Have you had a similar experience?

Can you remember a time before you landed in the wilderness when your dream seemed on the verge of coming true? Were you excitedly making plans and working hard to prepare for a lifetime of happiness? Did you feel as if you had the world by the tail, that all the pieces were falling into place and nothing could stop you? And are you now feeling dazed and confused, wondering what in the world went wrong?

If so, this chapter is especially for you. My goal here is to convince you to keep your dream alive as you travel the hard road before you. Why? Because your dream will give you strength and keep you going when you're tempted to quit. In addition, your dream could well be God-given. It just might be something He has big plans for—something He is planning to bless and to use at just the right time.

Oh yes, it would be easy to let your dream die. It would be easy to assume your painful circumstances somehow prove God never liked your dream in the first place. But that isn't necessarily true. In fact, I'm convinced God included Caleb's story in Scripture to refute that very notion. You see, Caleb's dream was deferred, but it wasn't defeated. Forty-five years after it was so cruelly snatched from his grasp, he returned to the hill country of Hebron and made it his home. Don't discount the possibility that you could be in store for a similar outcome!

When you finally come to the end of your hard road, you could find that you, like Caleb, have come full circle. You could find yourself right back where you once stood, with your dream sitting right in front of you. Only the second time around it will probably look even more attractive, just as those fertile hills must have seemed even more beautiful to Caleb after his tour of duty in the wilderness. Don't we always appreciate things more when we've had to wait, work, and suffer for them?

But the key is to keep your dream alive until it has a chance to come true. Let me offer three simple suggestions that will help you do this.

Keep Talking About Your Dream

Let me call your attention to a tiny but critical aspect of Caleb's story that most people completely overlook. It's found in a few key words that are tucked into a single verse in Joshua 14. The Israelites' forty-year hike through the wilderness is behind them, they have finally entered the Promised Land, and the time has come to divvy up the territory among the tribes. Caleb is a spry and feisty octogenarian who has waited patiently for one last chance to make his dream come true, and he realizes the time has come. With a spring in his step and his jaw firmly set, he marches up to Joshua (who had taken over for Moses) and gives an impassioned speech that concludes with the following request:

> I'm asking you to give me the hill country that the LORD promised
> me. You will remember that as scouts we found the Anakites living
> there in great, walled cities. But if the LORD is with me, I will drive
> them out of the land, just as the LORD said. (Josh. 14:12)

Most people are so captivated by the emotional speech of this die-hard dreamer that they fail to recognize a stunning detail that is revealed before Caleb even opens his mouth. Look carefully at verse 6:

> A delegation from the tribe of Judah, led by Caleb son of
> Jephunneh the Kenizzite, came to Joshua at Gilgal.

Do you see it?

It's the simple but telling fact that Caleb wasn't alone when he approached Joshua with his request. It says he showed up with a delegation. Maybe there were a dozen guys or perhaps a hundred. The point is, Caleb had obviously been talking about his dream. Knowing Caleb, I wouldn't be surprised if those poor guys had been hearing about it for all forty of the years they spent in the wilderness. But apparently, they didn't mind. Caleb's enthusiasm must have been so irresistible that they caught the vision themselves. At some point along the way, *his* dream became *their* dream. As a result, they were lined up behind him, ready to help him make it come true!

One of the best ways to keep your dream alive is to talk it up. But be careful! Some people are not dreamers or visionaries and will laugh at you. Others may be bitter because their own dreams have died and could try to tear yours down out of jealousy. And then there's always the chronic pessimist who thinks he's doing you a favor by enumerating all the reasons why your dream will probably never come true. Believe me, such people are out there. In my book *The Caleb Quest* (Nelson, 2004), I devote an entire chapter to the assassins that stalk our dreams. They can be your enemies or your friends. Yes, even your own family members can kill your dreams if they don't understand your passion or agree with your goals.

But if you know someone who shares your dreaming spirit, who loves you, and who has a dream or two of his own, by all means, talk to that person about your dream. You will find that just talking about it helps you shape and define it more clearly in your mind. And the person you're talking to could offer some keen insights that fuel your enthusiasm even more. Best of all, by talking up your dream, you just might find what Caleb found: a whole lot of people who are willing to help you make it happen. At the very least, as long as you're talking about your dream, it will keep living and breathing.

Keep Praying About Your Dream

There's an old story about a man who was shipwrecked on a deserted island. His boat was damaged badly enough that he couldn't repair it, so he dragged his few possessions onto the beach, sat on the sand, and watched for a ship or a plane to come by and rescue him. When a full day passed without any sign of either one, he decided he had better build some sort of shelter. So he gathered some bamboo poles, cut down some palm fronds, and tied them together with some vines. It wasn't the Ritz, but at least it was enough to keep him dry.

Several days later, a nearby storm spawned a lightning strike that set his little makeshift hut on fire. Horrified, he quickly started throwing sand on the flames and ran down to the surf to gather what little water he could in a small container. By the time the fire was extinguished, the hut was mostly destroyed, and the man, completely exasperated, sat on the ground and cried, "Why, God?" He bellowed, "Why are You doing this to me?"

Suddenly, he thought he heard the distant hum of a small airplane. Scrambling to his feet, he scanned the skies from one horizon to the other. Sure enough, off in the distance, he could see a small plane that appeared to be coming toward the island. Moments later, the plane landed and the pilot climbed out. The castaway embraced him and immediately began talking about all the hardships he'd faced. The pilot simply said, "Well, it's a good thing you decided to send up that smoke signal. Otherwise, I would never have known you were here."

I can't begin to count the times I have behaved just like that castaway. Something bad happens, and I get so busy trying to deal with the fallout that I forget to send up a signal for help. More times than I can count, I've had to sheepishly apologize to God for taking so long to come to Him in prayer. Then I always tell myself (and Him) that I'm not going to make the mistake again. But I do. It never fails.

For that reason, I have often felt that James 4:2 was written just for me. It says, "The reason you don't have what you want is that you don't ask God for it." Even now, as I'm copying the words of that verse into this manuscript, they sting a little. I know they point to one of my biggest weaknesses. There's no telling how many blessings I've missed out on over the years because I failed to send up a signal.

If your hard road has put your dream on hold or in jeopardy, you should be praying. Specifically, I can think of two things you should be praying for.

First, you should be praying for the strength to endure. Do you remember the story of George Washington and his men at Valley Forge? In case you're a little fuzzy on the details, let me refresh them for you.

After losing two key battles against the British, General Washington and his men were exhausted and demoralized. Suddenly, their dream of establishing an independent nation seemed in dire jeopardy. So they retreated to Valley Forge, where they planned to spend the winter recovering and regrouping. However, that winter was one of the coldest in history. Temperatures dropped far below zero, creating excruciating conditions for the soldiers, many who were inadequately clothed and even barefoot. The men lived in small huts and had to sleep in shifts because there weren't enough blankets to go around. While one group slept, the others sat huddled by the fires that burned constantly throughout the camp.

General Washington did what he could to maintain discipline, but it was his wife, Martha, who did more than anyone else to help those beleaguered soldiers survive. Every day, she walked from tent to tent and from bed to bed, stopping to pray for the men. She prayed for God's mercy and that He would give them the strength to endure the brutal cold and be victorious come spring. About a third of them died that winter, but the rest pulled themselves together and went out and won the war that gave birth to a new nation.[1]

Right now, you need to be praying for endurance. You need to be asking God for the strength to hang in there until this cold, hard winter you're going through is over. Why? Because there is an ebb and flow to life. Times of blessing and opportunity often follow right on the heels of our most difficult experiences. That's what David was getting at when he said, "Weeping may go on all night, but joy comes with the morning" (Ps. 30:5). At this moment, the biggest danger to your dream could be the temptation you feel to give up. You should be praying like mad for the strength to endure.

Second, you should be praying for God to bless your dream and make it a reality. And I say that knowing full well that you may not feel comfortable doing such a thing. A lot of people feel that such a prayer would be selfish and, therefore, offensive to God. But before you buy into that notion, stop and think about Hannah.

First Samuel 1 tells us that Hannah's hard road was barrenness during her prime childbearing years. In a culture where a woman's worth was measured largely by her ability to bear children, Hannah couldn't conceive. That, of course, was bad enough, but her heartache was intensified by the fact that her husband's other wife, Peninnah, had no trouble at all getting pregnant. A friend of mine who fathered three kids in four and a half years used to joke that all he had to do was wink at his wife from across the room and she would get pregnant. Apparently, that was Peninnah's situation. And oh, did she love to rub it in! Verse 7 says she made fun of Hannah for being childless, and that Hannah was often so hurt that she was reduced to tears and unable to eat. Can't you just imagine how some of those conversations must have unfolded?

PENINNAH: Hannah, would you be a dear and watch the baby while I run down to the creek and wash out a few things?

HANNAH: Well, I . . .

PENINNAH: If you'd rather not, I understand. I know my kids must be a constant reminder of your inadequacies. On the other hand, babysitting is probably the closest you're ever going to get to feeling like a mother.

I've often thought that Hannah probably deserves a medal simply for *not* punching Peninnah's lights out. To her credit, though she was completely distraught by Peninnah's hateful remarks, she took another approach to the problem.

She prayed.

She pleaded with God to make her dream of motherhood come true.

She apparently didn't worry about whether such a request would offend God. She simply poured her heart out to Him (1 Sam. 1:11), and He responded by giving her a baby boy. And not just a run-of-the-mill baby boy. He gave her a child with amazing gifts. A child that grew up to become one of the greatest heroes of the Old Testament. His name was Samuel.

So I would have to argue with anyone who says it's wrong to pray for your dream to come true. I would be much more inclined to say that it's wrong *not* to pray for it. Again, the Bible says we do not have things because we do not ask for them. And one of my favorite verses, Psalm 37:4, says, "Take delight in the LORD, and he will give you your heart's desires." Rather than assuming the futility of praying for our dreams, I would tend to agree with Alfred, Lord Tennyson, who said, "More things are wrought by prayer than this world dreams of."

You can keep your dream alive by constantly talking and praying about it. And then there's one more thing you can do.

Keep Moving Toward Your Dream

You probably know Phil Keaggy as a wonderful guitarist and songwriter. What you may not know is that Phil and his wife, Bernadette, once traveled a road so difficult it's almost impossible for anyone who hasn't been there to imagine. And trust me, very few people have been there. Thankfully.

It was 1975. Phil and Bernadette had been married almost two years when they learned that their dream of becoming parents was going to come true. Like most young couples, they were thrilled to the point of being giddy. They had a ball making plans and loved going to the doctor together and listening to the baby's heartbeat. With the nip of fall in the air, the holidays just around the corner, and a little Keaggy on the way, their spirits couldn't have been any higher.

But on November 1, their happy journey led to a Road Closed sign, and this left them facing a detour that led straight into the wilderness.

It was a Sunday and they were at church. Phil was leading the singing when Bernadette began feeling uncomfortable. It was way too soon to be going into labor, but she was definitely having contractions. They called the doctor, but he didn't seem alarmed. These things happen, he suggested, and encouraged her to call again the next morning if she was still feeling some discomfort. But almost as soon as she hung up the phone, the pain became excruciating. Suddenly, Bernadette lay wincing in the car as Phil made the twenty-five-minute drive to the hospital.

What happened next was not unlike what you might see on a television hospital drama. Medical professionals calmly but urgently prepared Bernadette for the arrival of a baby that simply wasn't going to wait any longer. What they didn't know as they hustled about was that they were minutes away from a huge surprise. You see, Bernadette was about to give birth to not one . . . not two . . . but three little boys! Sadly, at twenty-two weeks, the little guys just weren't strong enough to survive. The first two were stillborn and the third lived only a few minutes.

But for the briefest of moments, their three perfect little bodies, exquisitely formed down to the tiniest detail, lay on Bernadette's stomach. She ran her fingers lightly over their pale skin and stroked their hair as tears ran down her face. Then a nurse stepped in to do her unhappy duty. The last time Bernadette saw her sons, the nurse was wheeling them out of the room on a gurney.

Over the next couple of years, two more pregnancies ended in tragedy. First, Ryan was born at twenty-six weeks and two and a half pounds. He quickly developed hyaline membrane disease, which caused his lungs to stop working. Then in 1977, after seeking counsel from doctors who specialized in difficult pregnancies, Phil and Bernadette tried again, but the pregnancy ended in a miscarriage.

I can't even begin to imagine the heartache they must have felt after losing five babies. I've known people who've been emotionally and spiritually ruined by far less. But the Keaggys' faith, shaken as it must have been, carried them through. Phil continued to make music while they trusted God and nurtured the fragile hope that someday, somehow, God would give them a healthy baby.

Finally, a doctor who specialized in high-risk pregnancies determined that Bernadette's inability to carry a child to full term could likely be fixed with a simple surgical procedure. That procedure, which was performed at the end of the fourth month of her next pregnancy, made it possible for Bernadette to give birth to Alicia Marguerite, a perfectly formed, five-pound nine-ounce girl.

But that wasn't all God had in store for the faithful couple.

On February 14, 1984, Olivia Anne was born.

And then, in 1987, little Ian joined the family![2]

When I think of the Keaggys' story, I'm struck by the fact that they kept moving relentlessly in the direction of their dream. They could easily have given up after the first few failed pregnancies and no one would have blamed them. But no, they kept moving forward. They kept digging into the mystery of their babies' deaths. They talked to experts and consulted specialists. Walking by faith (and sometimes taking baby steps), they kept looking for answers and finally managed to close the gap between themselves and their dream's fulfillment.

Right now, you must understand that the distance between you and the fulfillment of your dream can grow a little smaller every day if you keep taking steps in the right direction. You may not be able to take big steps. Indeed, the hard road you're traveling may make even the smallest steps very difficult. But if even a little progress can be made, make it.

Not long ago, I read about a thirty-three-year-old woman who graduated from college. What made her story newsworthy was that she had been in a near-fatal accident as a teenager and came out of it with severe disabilities. From that point on, even the simplest movements, such as those required to brush her teeth or comb her hair, were almost impossibly difficult. Yet, she refused to give up her dream of being a college graduate. Against all odds, she enrolled in school and began by taking just one class. Finally, more than twelve years later, she got her degree.

While you're traveling your hard road, if you have an opportunity to move even one inch closer to your dream, do it. You see, inches add up. They turn into feet, yards, and miles. Then someday, when you come to the end of your wilderness, you could break into the clear and find yourself standing right on your dream's doorstep.

Before I move on, let me just say that I realize this particular chapter might have come into your hands a little too late. I recognize the possibility that your dream is already dead and buried. Maybe there was a time when it was alive and well, but you allowed it to die when you realized the path of your life was taking a turn into the wilderness. Maybe you assumed that hard roads and dreams just don't go together. Perhaps it seemed silly to keep such hopes alive when all the forces of eternity seemed to be conspiring against you.

If that's the case, it may be time to resurrect your dream—to roll the stone away from the tomb where it's buried and bring it back out into the sunshine. Because dreams do come true. Not just in fairy tales or Disney movies, but for real people. Yes, even hard-road travelers. Caleb and the Keaggys are proof. Someday you could be, too. Imagine someone pointing to *you* as an example of why a dream should never be allowed to die.

Wouldn't that be something?

Joshua then commanded the leaders of Israel, "Go through the camp and tell the people to get their provisions ready. In three days you will cross the Jordan River and take possession of the land the LORD *your God has given you."*

—JOSHUA 1:10–11

When You Come
to the Jordan, Cross It

Make the most of every opportunity.
—EPHESIANS 5:16

You've heard it said that opportunity knocks only once. Obviously, that is sometimes the case or such a saying would never have earned cliché status in our culture. But it isn't always true, and the Israelites are the perfect example.

After blowing their first chance to cross the Jordan and enter the Promised Land, God gave them a second opportunity four decades later. And, as you would expect after years of suffering in the wilderness, they were more than eager to do it. In fact, the following passage reveals a level of enthusiasm that borders on the ridiculous.

They answered Joshua, "We will do whatever you command us, and we will go wherever you send us. We will obey you just as we obeyed Moses. And may the LORD your God be with you as he was with Moses. Anyone who rebels against your word and does not obey your every command will be put to death. So be strong and courageous!" (Josh. 1:16–18)

I know those words aren't supposed to be funny, but I have to smile when I read them. They remind me of how my daughter used to react as a child when her mother or I was forced to take action against her rebellious behavior. The vigorous dusting of the seat of her pants always transformed her into a model child (at least temporarily). Naturally, some whimpering had to be done first. But in no time she would be all lovey-dovey, climbing all over us and hugging our necks. And if we even suggested that she should clean her room or pick up her toys, it was as if she were shot out of a rifle. She couldn't get to it fast enough.

Ah, the sweet rewards of posterior percussion!

(Oh, how I wish more parents would try it!)

At any rate, the Israelites, having had their britches dusted by their heavenly Father, were cocked and ready to fire. They were so fired up, I can almost picture the entire nation down in a sprinter's three-point stance, just waiting for Joshua to give the signal to charge!

But there's a lesson here, and we must not miss it.

When God brings you to the edge of your wilderness and offers you a way out, take it. Don't allow fear to paralyze you, which is what the Israelites did the first time around and what a lot of people do today.

Like Carol, for example.

She was married to an abusive, adulterous husband. Finally, after years of living every woman's worst nightmare, she was granted a divorce. But that didn't end her struggle. Suddenly single again, she found herself battling loneliness. She felt like the proverbial "fifth wheel" in social situations. And though she had no real evidence to support the notion, she suddenly felt as though the people in her church viewed her as a spiritual failure. But the worst of it was the guilt. She'd been raised to believe that it was a woman's job to make her man happy, so her ex-husband's hateful accusations continually splashed in her mind like waves against a rocky shore. Even though her friends all assured her she was mistaken, she somehow couldn't shake the feeling that she was responsible for the disaster her marriage had become.

And then she met Herb.

Herb was a strong Christian, a successful businessman, attractive enough to turn the majority of female heads, and a widower. Everybody (most of all, Herb) felt that their meeting and mutual attraction was ordained by God and held some sort of higher purpose. It seemed to be a match made in heaven. Carol even admitted that she saw in Herb all the qualities she could ever want in a husband. But when he asked her to marry him, she refused. She loved him, but the very thought of entrusting her body and soul to another man terrified her. She said that if somehow things didn't work out, she didn't think she could survive another divorce.

Carol had followed a long, hard road through a dark, scary wilderness, and everyone who knew her (including her pastor) could see that God had been faithful in leading her to her very own Jordan—to the very edge of a wonderful new life with a man who would love her the way a woman ought to be loved. But when the time came to cross over, she couldn't find the courage to do it.

Someday, you may find yourself in a similar situation.

Like Carol, you might be terrified of a new relationship that would end your loneliness forever. You might be afraid of a career change that would solve your financial struggles, an operation that would cure your health problems, or even a breakup that would finally set you free from a dysfunctional relationship.

Or maybe you're already there.

Maybe, even as you read these words, you're camped on the banks of your very own Jordan, looking across the water at a better life. Perhaps you can even look down and see the footprints of other happy souls who have crossed before you. Maybe you can see them on the other side, shouting and waving to you to come on across and join the party. But for some reason, you just can't make yourself take that first step.

In this chapter, I want to encourage you to do it, once and for all. But before you do, I'd like to offer three suggestions.

Be Thoughtful

No doubt part of your reluctance is that you fear the unseen and the unknown. From your vantage point, the opposite shore of your Jordan looks perfectly peachy. But you're wondering if there are devils lurking farther inland—perhaps hiding in the bushes just out of sight. You know appearances can be deceiving. You've already learned the painful truth that all that glitters is not gold. So naturally, you're afraid you might be walking into a trap.

Good for you!

There's nothing wrong with having your guard up. In fact, the Bible commands us to be alert (1 Peter 5:8), careful (Eph. 5:15), and discerning (1 Cor. 12:3). And it gives us stories like the one about the prodigal son to show us what happens when people go running off into the sunset without carefully considering the consequences of their actions.

Let me suggest three questions you ought to ask yourself as you stand on the banks of your Jordan and look across at what could be your Promised Land.

Question #1: Having studied, what is my Bible telling me? Paul said that all Scripture is inspired by God and useful to "teach us what is true" (2 Tim. 3:16). That's really what you're looking for, isn't it? Aren't you looking for a way to determine if the treasure you see on the other side of your Jordan is the real deal?

Well, then, get out your Bible and start digging. Or, if you don't know where to begin, ask a more Scripture-savvy friend, or perhaps your pastor, to help you. I'm confident you'll find some Bible passages that will speak to your situation. Even though a couple of thousand years have passed since the last Bible book was written, the Scriptures are amazingly relevant. I've yet to find a single problem the Scriptures don't address, either directly or indirectly.

Question #2: Having prayed, what is the Spirit telling me? James 1:5 says, "If you need wisdom—if you want to know what God wants you to do—ask him, and he will gladly tell you." The question is, *how* will He tell you?

I always get a little nervous when people start talking about hearing messages from God. The words "God told me to" have been used to justify everything from divorce to terrorism. Rather than speaking in an audible voice, I believe God will simply turn your heart toward or away from whatever it is you're questioning. A good verse to keep in mind is Colossians 3:15: "Let the peace that comes from Christ rule in your hearts." When you've searched the Scriptures and prayed, you'll probably start feeling a sense of peace about one choice or the other.

Question #3: Having listened, what are my friends telling me? Proverbs 19:20 says, "Get all the advice and instruction you can." That means you aren't quite done when you've searched the Scriptures and prayed, because God also uses people to point us in the right direction.

But which people?

It seems to me that some of the loudest voices in our world are giving some of the worst advice. I am appalled at the amount of false doctrine that is spewing out over the airwaves and showing up on Christian bookstore shelves. Therefore, I would encourage you never to choose your counselor based on glitz, glamour, or popularity. Just because a person has a best-selling book, a television program, or a prominent position in a high-profile church doesn't mean he (or she) is wise. Also, steer clear of coworkers, family members, or acquaintances who have not demonstrated the ability to manage their own lives well. (It always amazes me how the most messed-up people are often the first to tell you what you ought to do.) Instead, listen to that person you know personally who has consistently demonstrated a heart for God and whose life reflects a long track record of good decisions. Proverbs 15:7 says, "Only the wise can give good advice."

Finally, after you've prayed, studied the Scriptures, listened to the advice of your friends, and then taken some time to mull it all over, you should be ready to make a decision. If, at that point, there are no compelling reasons for you to hold back, then go ahead. Cross your Jordan. But . . .

Be Careful

Even if it is God's will for you to move into a wonderful new stage of life, that doesn't mean your troubles are over. Moses reminded the Israelites of this fact in Deuteronomy 9:1–2 as they prepared to cross the Jordan for the second time:

> Hear, O Israel! Today you are about to cross the Jordan River to occupy the land belonging to nations much greater and more powerful than you. They live in cities with walls that reach to the sky! They are strong and tall—descendants of the famous Anakite giants. You've heard the saying, "Who can stand up to the Anakites?"

If I had been in Moses' sandals, I'm sure I wouldn't have mentioned these facts. I would have been afraid of scaring the people into another mutiny like the one that got them sent off into the desert in the first place. Rather, I would have focused on the milk and honey aspects of the land. I would have held up a big fat watermelon and said, "Look what we're going to be eating! We'll even be able to organize a nationwide seed-spitting contest!" But no, Moses chose to bring up the Anakites.

The lesson is obvious: You can never let your guard down, even after you've left the wilderness. You may feel as though you've stepped into a utopian paradise and left your troubles far behind, but that will never be completely true this side of heaven. Paul said, "If you think you are standing strong, be careful" (1 Cor. 10:12).

David's life illustrates this perfectly.

You may remember that his defeat of Goliath made him an instant celebrity. And why not? As little more than a kid, he did something the entire Israelite army couldn't find the gumption to do. The downside was that Saul, the king (and the guy who should have dealt with the Goliath situation long before David ever showed up), became insanely jealous and started trying to eliminate David. Some of his attempts were subtle, such as sending David off to fight in the hope that he would be killed in battle (1 Sam. 18:25). And as I mentioned in Chapter 9, other attempts were brazen, such as sending a team of killers to ambush him as he walked out of his house (1 Sam. 19:11). Finally, it became apparent that Saul had completely lost his mind and would stop at nothing to see David dead.

And so began David's hard-road journey.

He fled into the wilderness, where he lived as a fugitive for several months. During this time we see both the best and the worst of David. At times, he showed tremendous faith and respect for

God's sovereignty, such as the two occasions when he had a chance to kill Saul in his sleep, but refused (1 Sam. 24; 26). Yet, at other times, he seemed to completely forget about God, such as the time he visited Ahimelech the priest and told a whole series of lies (1 Sam. 21:1–9). That was a terrible failure, to be sure, and some commentators love to clobber David with the club of self-righteousness. But don't forget what I pointed out in Chapter 2, that Satan lurks along the hard roads of life and sets many traps. I've yet to find a person who could make it all the way through a hostile wilderness without making a misstep or two. So don't feel bad if you've stumbled a few times.

Finally, Saul was killed in a battle with the Philistines, and David's fugitive days were over. In no time, he found himself reigning as the king of Judah. That's a pretty good promotion, wouldn't you say? From cave dweller to palace dweller. From sleeping on the cold, hard ground to sleeping on a goose-down mattress. From dodging spears to eating grapes from the hand of a pretty young maiden. Yes indeed, with the wilderness behind him, he could finally relax. All his troubles were over.

Or were they?

David's personal circumstances had improved dramatically, but there were still many problems to be dealt with, such as the civil war that raged between Judah and the remaining tribes of Israel. And even after peace was made and the two groups were united, David found himself battling temptation (remember Bathsheba?) and facing an uprising that was led by his own son, Absalom.

So you see, just crossing from the wilderness into the Promised Land—or moving from a cave to a palace—doesn't mean you can afford to let your guard down. Yes, your personal circumstances may improve. But as long as you're living in this fallen world, there will be dangers.

As I think along these lines, I'm reminded of a preacher friend of mine who found himself in a difficult ministry. The church was strife-torn, and he literally made himself sick trying to keep the people from scratching one another's eyes out. His stress level was off the charts, he was suffering from hypertension, and he had developed an ulcer. He tried on several occasions to relocate, but for one reason or another, none of the churches he applied for offered him a position. If ever a man was stuck in the wilderness, he was.

Then one day the call that he had been praying for finally came. A church with a fine reputation felt that his gifts matched perfectly with its needs and offered him the position of preaching minister. Naturally, he was on cloud nine. He said he felt as though he'd been granted a pardon from death row. Without a doubt, he'd come to his Jordan and was going to waste no time crossing it.

But one Sunday, very early in his new ministry, he discovered that there were Anakites in the land.

He happened to make a comment about homosexuality being a sin. Suddenly a woman who was sitting just a few rows from the front got up and walked out—stormed out, would be more like it. Stormed out while casting an angry glare over her shoulder at the preacher, would be even *more* like it. She literally glowed with rage, he said.

Come to find out, the woman had a homosexual son and was supersensitive on the subject. Of course, the new preacher had no idea. He was merely fulfilling his calling as a communicator of God's Word. But from that day forward, he had a "walled city" to contend with right there in his new congregation. The woman resisted his influence on every level and openly criticized his every move. She became, to quote Paul, that preacher's "thorn in the flesh."

Was he sorry he moved?

No.

Was his overall life better in that new congregation?

Yes.

Would he have made the move all over again if given the chance?

Absolutely.

But the experience was a vivid reminder that there can be no utopian existence in a fallen world. Just as every rose has its thorns, so every life situation will have its challenges. Remember this as you gather up your gear and prepare to cross your Jordan.

Be Hopeful

My final suggestion is that you cross your Jordan with some bounce in your step. I often think it must disappoint God to see His people tiptoeing around as if they're afraid they're going to step on a land mine. Yes, there are good reasons to be careful wherever we go, but Paul makes it clear that God has not given us a spirit of fear and timidity (2 Tim. 1:7). When we're convinced we're doing God's will, we ought to be the most upbeat and optimistic people in the world.

Let me show you two wonderful pictures of God's care and protection that are both seen in the Israelites' transition from the wilderness to the Promised Land.

First, in Joshua 3, we find the story of the actual crossing of the Jordan River. Verse 15 mentions that it was the time of year when the river was overflowing its banks. I can relate to that because I grew up in rural southern Illinois. As a result of the spring rains, the Little Wabash River, which was barely more than fifty feet wide the rest of the time, was transformed into something more resembling Lake Michigan. Thousands of acres of farmland were completely swallowed up by its floodwaters. Fortunately, a system of levees, elevated roads, and bridges allowed traffic to move freely throughout the area. But in Joshua's time, there were no such advantages.

So God did a really cool thing.

He gave instructions for the priests to lead the march across the river while carrying the ark of the covenant. They were told to step into the water and then stop. When they did, the water parted. The Bible says it "piled up" at locations both up- and downstream, creating a dry bed for the nation to walk on (Josh. 3:16–17).

What a beautiful picture of God paving the way for His people. They couldn't set their feet on a spot He hadn't already prepared for them.

For the second picture, I need to take you back to the passage I quoted earlier, where Moses reminded the people that they were going to encounter giants and walled cities when they crossed the Jordan. It's important to note that he didn't stop there. He quickly added the following:

> But the LORD your God will cross over ahead of you like a devouring fire to destroy them. He will subdue them so that you will quickly conquer them and drive them out, just as the LORD has promised. (Deut. 9:3)

Have you ever seen a "devouring fire" up close? I did when I was in high school. The furniture store where I worked, and that I lived less than a block away from, caught fire in the middle of the night. I remember hearing sirens and getting up to look out the window. Though I couldn't see the store, the trees across the street were glowing orange as they reflected the light of the roaring flames. I hustled into my clothes and ran out into the street where I stood in awe. I could feel the heat on my skin as the flames literally swallowed up the back half of the building. A devouring flame is a terrifying thing, and that's what God promised to be for His people as they moved into the Promised Land.

So put the two pictures together: You have God preparing the ground for every step His people take. And moving ahead of them like a blowtorch to consume their enemies.

I see here a picture of the God who understands how hard it is for us to move into uncharted territory, even when it looks inviting. He understands that we are drawn to the familiar, even when it causes us pain. That's why people stay in abusive relationships, why they refuse to have corrective surgery that would dramatically improve the quality of their lives, and why they spend years slogging away in dead-end jobs. It's so easy to assume that everyone who comes to the Jordan will cross it, but it isn't true. The Israelites had two chances and ended up batting .500.

Understanding this tendency in human nature, God went above and beyond the call of duty to instill hope and confidence in the hearts of His people. In fact, He did everything for them except make the final decision. He left that up to them, as He always does.

There's a story about a woman who was having a bad dream. In the dream, a terrifying monster was chasing her and gaining ground. She didn't dare look back for fear of losing a step, but she could tell from the creature's ghastly noises that it would soon overtake her. Desperate, she turned down a dark alley, but was suddenly horrified to see that it was a dead end. She ran as far as she could, pressed her back against the wall, and watched the monster creep toward her. Impulsively, she said, "What are you going to do to me?" And the monster straightened up and answered, "It's up to you. It's your dream."

Obviously, we don't get to choose everything that happens in our lives. But there are some critical moments when God steps back and says, "It's up to you. It's your life." And one of those moments will come when you stand on the banks of your Jordan. He will be ready to escort you into your new life and help you face all its risks and dangers. Or you can do an about-face and head back into your wilderness.

It's up to you. It's your life.

Please do the right thing.

When you come to your Jordan, cross it.

When all the people were safely across the river, the LORD said to Joshua, "Now choose twelve men, one from each tribe. Tell the men to take twelve stones from where the priests are standing in the middle of the Jordan and pile them up at the place where you camp tonight."

So Joshua called together the twelve men and told them, "Go into the middle of the Jordan, in front of the Ark of the LORD your God. Each of you must pick up one stone and carry it out on your shoulder— twelve stones in all, one for each of the twelve tribes. We will use these stones to build a memorial. In the future, your children will ask, 'What do these stones mean to you?' Then you can tell them, 'They remind us that the Jordan River stopped flowing when the Ark of the LORD's covenant went across.' These stones will stand as a permanent memorial among the people of Israel."

—JOSHUA 4:1–7

Turn Your Trip into a Testimony

This will be your opportunity to tell them about me.
—MATTHEW 10:18

In 1990, I gave Marilyn a very special Christmas present. It was a written history of our life together. I started working on it in May of that year. I spent countless hours of my free time at the office, hunched over an electric typewriter, reliving our many fascinating experiences in my mind, and putting them down in a sort of marital autobiography. I was always afraid she might ask why I was spending all those extra hours in the office, but she never did. Bless her heart, she thought her husband was behind that closed door immersing himself in Scripture and seeking the Lord in prayer.

But on Christmas morning she found out I wasn't nearly as spiritual as she thought. It didn't matter, though. I was a hero, first, for having the idea, and second, for spending so much time on it. Our daughter, Michelle, who was twelve at the time, didn't share her mother's enthusiasm for the gift. In those days, if you couldn't wear it, eat it, or listen to it, an object held little value to her. But I'm not worried. One of these days, when Marilyn and I are gone, she will cherish those pages. They will enhance her memories of her parents.

Memorials are cherished in our culture, as evidenced by the fact that you see them everywhere. If you're married, the ring on your finger is a memorial—a reminder of the vows you made to your spouse. You probably also have photo albums in your home containing pictures of deceased relatives, or a collection of memorabilia that reflect your career path, or some souvenirs that remind you of the places you've visited on vacation. I'm guessing you also have some home movies, or perhaps your child's first pair of shoes bronzed and mounted like a trophy.

And that's just what's *inside* your house. When you step outside, you'll find even more memorials.

You may have a graduation tassel hanging from the rearview mirror of your car. You probably drive on streets that are named after important people who've had an impact on your community. You may drive past a cemetery on your way to work, or a courthouse where a World War I cannon is on display. Chances are, the Little League complex in your town bears a person's name, or the performing arts center, or the middle school, or the playground at the city park. Or maybe the town itself bears someone's name. I grew up in southern Illinois near towns named Samsville, Lawrenceville, Louisville, Johnsonville, and St. Francisville.

We love memorials!

But that's okay because God does too.

As soon as all the Israelites were safely across the Jordan, God gave instructions for them to build a memorial using twelve stones taken out of the dry riverbed. It was to stand as a testimony to future generations of the goodness and the power of God.

Likewise, when you've crossed your Jordan, you'll want to build a memorial. Not a physical monument made of stones, but a testimony you can share with the people you meet who may be traveling a similar road and in desperate need of encouragement. In fact, when all is said and done, this will likely be the most important result of your hard-road journey. It will give you the best opportunity you've ever had to make an impact on others for the Lord.

Do you remember what you learned in high-school science class about the four ways substances react to light? Some are *transparent*, which means light passes through them. Others are *translucent*, which means they scatter light. Still other substances are *opaque*, which means they block light. And then there are *mirrors*, which reflect light.

I'm sure you've noticed . . .

- There are lots of transparent people, who seem oblivious to the Light.

- There are countless translucent people, who make the Light very confusing.

- There are even more opaque people, who are dead-set against the Light.

- But, praise God, there are a few mirrorlike people who reflect the Light.

God has called us all to be mirrors, to reflect His Light to the world. The fact that you've been on a hard road and survived by walking with Him means you have a lot of Light to reflect.

The Power of a Story

A testimony is simply a story, and a story is a powerful thing. So powerful, in fact, that it was Jesus' favorite teaching tool. There were times when He lectured, used the question-and-answer method, or simply engaged in penetrating conversations. But by far, His favorite way of connecting with people was by telling stories. Matthew 13:34 says, "Jesus always used stories and illustrations like these when speaking to the crowds. In fact, he never spoke to them without using such parables."

The beauty of a story is that it gives life to the truth. Just think about the times you've sat through a class lecture or a sermon, feeling bored out of your mind. But as soon as the professor or the preacher said, "Let me tell you a story," you suddenly perked up and tuned in.

Several years ago, two motivational speakers, Jack Canfield and Mark Victor Hansen, decided to assemble their favorite inspirational stories into a single volume and try to get it published. When they finally got the manuscript prepared, they began offering it to all the big New York publishing houses. But the response was ice-cold. In the first month alone, they received thirty-three rejections. Over time, 140 publishers gave the manuscript a "thumbs-down." In fact, the authors' agent became so frustrated that he gave up on the book and stopped trying to sell it.

But Jack and Mark still believed in the project, so they went to the American Booksellers Association Convention and carried their manuscript from booth to booth, trying to find someone—*anyone*—who might be interested. Thankfully, they did. A man named Peter Vegso, president of Health Communications, Inc., caught the vision of the book and decided to give it wings.

And the rest, as they say, is history.

The manuscript ended up being titled *Chicken Soup for the Soul* and was published in June 1993. I don't have to tell you that the book turned into a series that took the publishing industry by storm. Chicken Soup books started appearing on best-seller lists all over the country and winning prestigious awards, prompting *Time* magazine to call the series the "publishing phenomenon of the decade." As of this writing, more than eighty million Chicken Soup books have been sold in thirty-seven languages.[1] I wouldn't be surprised if a few of those are in your home at this moment.

The point is, everybody loves a great story. We start reading them to our children even before they're fully able to understand them. We tell them around campfires and watch them on television. We turn the best ones into best-selling books and Hollywood blockbusters that earn hundreds of millions of dollars. And we preachers stuff our sermons full of them. Craig Brian Larson said, "Preachers crave illustrations [stories] like the thundering steam locomotives of yesteryear did coal."[2] And the reason is that we know how powerful they are.

The Power of a True Story

One of my favorite movies is *The Rookie*, starring Dennis Quaid as Jim Morris. As a young fireballing left-hander, Morris dreamed of someday pitching in the big leagues, but was forced to retire and go into coaching when he blew out his arm. One season, with the high school team he was coaching mired in last place, he offered his players a deal. If they could turn their season around and win the championship, he would try out for a major-league team. Amazingly, the team was transformed and went from worst to first, leaving Morris with the obligation of dragging his almost forty-year-old body to a major-league tryout camp. It seemed hopeless. Worse than hopeless, it seemed silly. But as a man of his word, he did it—and ended up becoming the oldest rookie in the majors.

The reason I love that movie is not just because it's about baseball, though that certainly helps. More than anything, I love it because it really happened. Jim Morris is not just the figment of some novelist's imagination. He's a real guy who actually did the things depicted in the movie. For that reason, every time I pop in the DVD and watch it, I'm forced to think about my own dreams and ask myself if, perhaps, there might be some I've given up on too soon.

You see, that's the power of a *true* story. It has the uncanny ability to shine a searchlight into your soul. It compels you to ask questions you might rather not ask or face realities you might rather not face. I believe this is the real reason why Mel Gibson's movie *The Passion of the Christ* was so difficult to watch. Yes, the violence was intense, but far more intense for me was the experience of having my tidy, spit-polished image of the Crucifixion completely ripped apart and seeing in vivid detail exactly what *my* sins did to *my* Lord.

But a true story not only shines a searchlight into your soul; it also shines a spotlight on the wonderful and amazing things God is capable of doing. And this, it seems to me, is critical. Isn't it true that our lives can become so difficult that we lose sight of God? Isn't it true that sometimes the challenge of just putting one foot in front of the other is so all-consuming that there's no room for anything else on the radar screen? This is why Paul cautioned us not only to think about things here on earth, but also to lift our eyes and focus on the things above (Col. 3:1–2). It's essential that we stay connected to the Person who is far and away our greatest ally in the struggle. The great value of a true story is that it places a finger under the hard-road traveler's chin and gently pushes up. Unlike fiction, it forces the person to ask, "Could God do something like that for me?"

The Power of Your Story

So what about your story? Could you tell it in a way that would minister to others? Perhaps you don't see yourself as a great communicator. Maybe you lack a platform. Or maybe you think your story isn't dramatic enough to be of interest to people.

Let me address these concerns one at a time.

"I'm Not a Great Communicator"

Nobody's suggesting that you become a motivational speaker and travel the country, sharing your testimony with church groups and corporations. Some people do that, of course, but 99.9 percent of the hard-road survivors in this world never do. They're simply ordinary people who do ordinary things for a living. They will never write a book, give a speech, or be interviewed by the media. Instead, they will share their stories in the most casual of situations, mostly one-on-one. And for that reason, it is not necessary that they be polished orators.

It's perfectly acceptable for you to be a part of that 99.9 percent. However, that doesn't mean you shouldn't spend some time working on your testimony. The better organized it is and the more comfortable you feel telling it, the more effective it will be. Remember, even the most naturally gifted public speakers spend countless hours crafting their presentations. So certainly, there is no excuse for not putting some time into yours.

The big thing to remember is that your testimony is simply your story. It doesn't have to be a sermon. It doesn't have to be theological. It doesn't have to answer all the difficult questions people might feel inclined to ask. All it has to do is show how the Lord helped you as you walked with Him along your hard road.

"I Have No Platform"

You may not stand behind a pulpit on Sunday, host a radio show, or employ an agent to field all the calls you're getting from Oprah and Jay Leno. But trust me. You *do* have a platform for your message.

Your platform is simply the life God has given you to live in your own little corner of the world. There, you have family, friends, and acquaintances—people who didn't learn about your hard-road journey on the evening news. Rather, they learned about it because they happened to be standing close to you when the explosion happened. Those may well be the only people you'll ever witness to. Whatever you do, don't underestimate their importance.

In Mark 5, we find the chilling story of a demon-possessed man who was terrorizing the entire land of the Gadarenes. He was a wild-eyed creature who lived among the tombs and howled like a banshee. In the interest of public safety, some brave souls banded together and tried to bind him in chains and haul him away like an animal, but his superhuman strength enabled him to snap the chains and tear the shackles from his wrists. Day after day, his bloodcurdling screams could be heard throughout the area as he bruised and tore his flesh with whatever sharp rocks he could find. The man was, in the most literal sense, a monster.

But one day, he encountered Jesus and was delivered. Understandably, he was all set to follow Jesus to the ends of the earth. But Jesus forbade him with a telling statement. He said, "No, go home to your friends, and tell them what wonderful things the Lord has done for you and how merciful he has been" (Mark 5:19).

Think about it.

Right there, Jesus had the perfect opportunity to give that guy a gigantic platform. He could have made him the star of His traveling evangelistic team. Jesus could have taken him along and put him front and center at every stop along the way. He could have made the man exhibit A in His campaign to show the world the power of God. But He didn't. Instead, He sent him home. Back to his own little corner of the world. Back to the people who knew him before the path of his life took such an ugly turn.

Here's the bottom line on this platform business.

Yes, we need big platform people. No one in his right mind would deny that. But we also need little platform people. We need ordinary folks who lead ordinary lives to tell *extra*ordinary stories about God's goodness. Why? Because they are the only witnesses some people will pay attention to. Many people are suspicious of big platform preachers, authors, and celebrities, and rightfully so. Some over the years have proved to not be so trustworthy. But when they hear a friend or a neighbor who has nothing to gain talking about God's goodness, it means something.

"My Story Isn't Dramatic Enough"

It's true that the more dramatic a story is, the wider its audience will be. But it would be a grave mistake to measure the effectiveness of any testimony by the size of its audience. Many people may be drawn to a highly dramatic story merely out of curiosity or because of its sheer entertainment value. For example, a true story about a person shipwrecked on a deserted island might make a terrific read, but how many people have ever been in that situation? You see, most people do not live highly dramatic lives. Most people have never had an experience worthy of being turned into a book or a movie. They may read books or watch movies about people who have had such experiences, but that doesn't mean they can relate to the stories on a personal level.

Therefore, the best way to measure the value of a testimony is not by the size of its audience, but by the impact it has on the people who hear it. If your story helps even one person stay faithful to the Lord—or perhaps return to the Lord—then it has had an eternal impact.

Here's something I truly believe. I'll admit that I don't have "book, chapter, and verse" to support what I'm about to say, but I believe this based on many years of serving the Lord and people. It's my conviction that if you have a valid, Christ-centered testimony you're willing to share, God will bring people across your path who need to hear it. If, for example, God has helped you endure and overcome the pain of a miscarriage, I can almost guarantee that at some point, you're going to meet a couple who has recently had the same experience and needs your help. I've seen it happen again and again. So often, in fact, that I always tell the hard-road travelers in the church I serve that God is preparing them for ministry. "Who, me?" they ask. And I say, "Yes, you. One of these days you're going to meet someone who desperately needs to know exactly what you're learning here today."

So don't feel intimidated because you lack the gift of gab. Don't feel powerless because you're a nobody in the eyes of the world. And don't feel inferior because your story seems a little boring compared to some others you've heard. Just quietly live your life in the little corner of the world where God has placed you, and be ready at all times to tell people what wonderful things the Lord has done for you and how merciful He has been. Just by doing that, you could save somebody's life.

As I bring this chapter to a close, I want to tell you about Cheryl McGuinness.

For her, September 11, 2001, started like any other day, with a predawn good-bye kiss from her husband, Tom, who was heading off to his job as an American Airlines pilot. By midmorning, however, the day had become like no other. Terrifying pictures were being flashed across America's TV screens, and Cheryl was trying desperately to find out if Tom had been on either of the planes that had crashed into the World Trade Center. She knew he had been the instant she saw a big black car pull into her driveway. Five men got out. Four of them wore dark suits, and the fifth was a priest.

Four years have now come and gone since that terrible day. To her credit, Cheryl didn't fold herself up into the fetal position and withdraw from the human race, though I suspect she was tempted. Instead, she locked arms with the Lord and traveled her hard road with dignity and courage. And she turned her trip into a testimony. In her book, *Beauty Beyond the Ashes*, she says something you need to contemplate as you think about sharing your story with others:

> The results of my speaking ministry regularly take my breath away. All I'm doing is opening my mouth and sharing what God is doing in my life. How could something so simple make such an impact? At times I ask, "Am I worthy to be doing God's work? Why would he choose me to serve him?" And then I receive cards, notes, or e-mail messages from people telling me that something I shared touched them at their very point of need—and my questions evaporate.
>
> I don't feel worthy to be speaking in front of so many people, but I am grateful for the opportunities. The responses I receive feed me and bless me so much. They confirm to me that I am doing what God wants me to do. And they create a passion and excitement within me that keeps me going. Because I have this new purpose, I tend to do less looking back at what was and less looking ahead with painful feelings at what I don't have. Instead, I do more focusing on *what can be* as I continue to move ahead, trusting and serving the Lord.[3]

Read those last two sentences again.

Nobody needs a sense of purpose more than a hard-road traveler. In order to "move ahead, trusting and serving the Lord," you simply must see a purpose beyond your pain. Cheryl found her purpose in helping others, and you can too. As I said before, you may never stand on a stage and speak to thousands. You may never publish a best-selling book. You may never be invited to be a guest on *Oprah*. But if you'll just keep your eyes and ears open, God will bring someone across your path who desperately needs to know what you have learned. And when you share your story and see the relief and hope it brings, you'll know that your suffering was not in vain.

A Letter from Mark

Dear Reader,

Every time I walk into a Borders or a Barnes and Noble, I'm reminded that there are probably a good many more books in print than we actually need. That you decided to pick this one out of the lot and read it amazes me. I am truly thankful, and I hope you found it helpful.

I never believed this book would alter the course of Western civilization, but the longer I worked on it, the more I developed the feeling that God might be up to something even bigger than my vision. Little things kept happening that seemed to affirm the message. Often, they left me looking heavenward and feeling a sense of awe.

For example, I finished the story about Phil and Bernadette Keaggy's stillbirths and miscarriages on a Saturday evening. The very next day, a woman approached me at church and asked if we could speak privately. As soon as we stepped into my office, she began to well up. In a faltering voice, she told me that her daughter had just suffered her second miscarriage the day before and was despondent. "Can you suggest something I might tell her that would give her some hope?" she asked. I was able to share the

Keaggys' story in detail because it was so fresh in my mind, and the woman couldn't wait to get home and share it with her daughter.

There were many incidents like this, and every one was a reminder that God is always working, orchestrating the circumstances of our lives to see that we get what we need, when we need it. I sincerely hope this book came into your hands at just the right moment and that it offered just the help you needed.

If it did, I'd like for you to write and tell me. It will further strengthen my faith to know how God is using this project, but it will also give me some wonderful stories to tell as I travel the country and share the message of *Walking with God on the Road You Never Wanted to Travel*. Perhaps your story will be just the one some weary traveler needs to hear.

My e-mail address is markatteberry@aol.com.

Currently, I'm hard at work on my next Thomas Nelson book. When it's released, I'd be honored if you would meet me in its pages so we can continue our pursuit of God's truth together. Until then, let's keep walking with the Lord on whatever road He asks us to travel.

In His Love,
Mark

Questions for Group Discussion
or Personal Reflection

Strategy #1: Understand How You Wound Up
in the Wilderness

1. Think back to the time when you first realized the path of your well-planned life had veered off into the wilderness. What emotions did you feel at that moment? Are some of those emotions still lingering? How have they affected you?

2. Do you believe your wilderness journey is mostly your own fault, someone else's fault, or nobody's fault? Explain why you feel this way.

3. If you landed on a hard road primarily because of your own actions, what changes have you made in your general approach to life that will prevent you from making the same mistakes again?

4. If you landed on a hard road primarily because of someone else's actions, have you forgiven that person? If yes, what evidence could you give to prove it?

Strategy #2: Commit to Strict Obedience

1. Satan dogged the Israelites' steps as they wandered in the wilderness. Have you felt him dogging yours? Have you noticed an increase in temptation? Have you slipped into some bad habits and attitudes since your hard-road journey began? If so, how do you intend to take back that lost ground and defend yourself in the future?

2. The Bible teaches that it's your responsibility to mark out a straight path for your feet and stick to it (Prov. 4:25–26). What are you currently doing that is helping you accomplish that goal?

3. When you get a little lazy in your relationship with God, what kind of junk tends to accumulate in your life? How "junky" is your life at this moment? In what ways is the junk in your life making your hard road harder? What do you intend to do about this? When do you plan to start?

Strategy #3: Travel with a Friend

1. Is someone walking with you on your hard road? What is that person's relationship to you? Why do you think he (or she) is doing it?

2. If no one is walking with you, can you think of someone who might be willing? What qualities does that person possess that make you believe he (or she) would be a good companion?

3. If you have a faithful traveling companion, what have you done to show that person your love and appreciation?

4. Is there a hard-road traveler in your circle of acquaintances who desperately needs a traveling companion? Could you be that companion?

Strategy #4: Stay Positive

1. Your situation may be unpleasant, but in what ways could it be worse? Can you look around and see someone whose circumstances are more difficult than yours?

2. Are you sometimes guilty of assuming the worst? Can you think of a situation when your negative thinking robbed you of a blessing?

3. Pessimistic thinking shows a lack of trust in God. If you have a problem with pessimism, what is it about God that makes you feel you can't trust Him?

4. Romans 8:28 says that God causes all things to work together for the good of those who love Him and are called according to His purpose for them. How have you seen this verse proved true in your own life?

Strategy #5: Step over the Dead and Keep Going

1. The hard roads of life are lined with the graves of people who gave up hope and gave in to the devil. To what extent have you considered Satan's hatred of you? Have you been viewing him as a nuisance or an enemy? What have you done that proves you've been taking him seriously?

2. James 4:7 says that if we resist the devil, he will flee. What are some specific ways you could begin offering more resistance than you have in the past?

3. Can you identify any channels through which impurity is flowing into your life? If so, what steps can you take to stop that flow?

4. Do you have trouble focusing on the things above (Col. 3:1–2)? If so, what's the problem? Are you hanging out with the wrong people? Not giving enough attention to the Word? What, specifically, can you do to maintain more of an upward focus?

Strategy #6: Trust God to Meet Your Needs

1. When God provided manna for the Israelites, it was never too early and never too late. Can you relate a personal experience that illustrates God's perfect timing in meeting your needs?

2. Also, there was never too much manna and never too little. Have you sometimes been guilty of wanting more than you really needed and feeling a little bitter when you didn't get it? What is your standard in determining how much you need?

3. In Psalm 139:7 David said, "I can never escape from your spirit!" Can you name an unusual place where you had a powerful, unexpected encounter with God? What happened?

Strategy #7: Go at God's Pace

1. Can you think of a time when you took a shortcut and ended up suffering as a result? What happened? What did you learn from the experience?

2. Does God's pace frustrate you? Why do you believe He never seems to be in a hurry?

3. Are there people in your life who always seem to be in a hurry? Do you tend to adopt their mind-set when you're around them? What can you do to reduce their influence?

4. God said, "In quietness and confidence is your strength" (Isa. 30:15). What changes could you make in your daily life that would move you closer to the truth of this verse?

Strategy #8: Enjoy Every Oasis

1. Solomon said there is "a time to cry and a time to laugh. A time to grieve and a time to dance" (Eccl. 3:4). Have you done any laughing or dancing since you started your hard-road journey? If not, is it because you haven't had any chances, or because you haven't seized the chances you've had?

2. Can you name a person who has been like a refreshing oasis to you as you have traveled your hard road? What have you done to show that person your gratitude?

3. Can you think of someone who needs a refreshing oasis? Could you become that person's oasis? What, specifically, would you need to do to make that happen?

4. How many copies of the Bible do you own? How long has it been since you read one of them? Do you have a regular Bible-reading schedule? If not, what is keeping you from establishing one?

5. Jesus said, "If you are thirsty, come to me!" (John 7:37). Obviously, you went to Jesus when you became a Christian. But do you still go to Him on a daily basis for strength and nourishment? How, specifically, can you make Jesus more a part of your daily walk?

Strategy #9: Expect Detours

1. Have you encountered any detours on your hard road? What, specifically, has happened to make your journey longer than you originally thought it would be?

2. No doubt you were unhappy when you encountered the detour, but has anything good happened as a direct result of it?

3. Jacob learned some valuable lessons as he was being forced to take a long detour on his way to marrying Rachel. What has your detour taught you about life? What has it taught you about yourself?

Strategy #10: Worship on the Way

1. Has worship become difficult for you since you landed on your hard road? If so, explain.

2. Have you, at any point, dropped out of fellowship with your church as a result of your hard-road journey? If so, why did you do this? What effect has it had on your faith? How has it affected your relationships with your Christian friends?

3. Ezra said, "God protects all those who worship Him, but his fierce anger rages against those who abandon him" (Ezra 8:22). In light of this statement, do you believe it is reasonable to expect God to bless you if you are not devoting yourself to worship?

4. When Elijah was depressed, it took an encounter with God and some good news to restore him. Could that be what you need right now? If so, can you think of a better place to find it than in a corporate worship service where God has promised to be present (Matt. 18:20)?

5. If you have dropped out of church, have you thought about the impact your decision could have on others? What do you think that impact might be?

Strategy #11: Keep Your Dreams Alive

1. What is your dream? Was there a time before you landed in the wilderness when it seemed on the verge of coming true?

2. What is the status of your dream now? Have you abandoned it completely? Or do you still intend to pursue it? Have you shared it with anyone? Do you know someone who might be willing to help you chase it?

3. When was the last time you prayed about your dream? The Bible says we do not have because we do not ask (James 4:2). In the spirit of Hannah, who prayed fervently for her dream of becoming a mother, are you willing to start lifting your dream up to God every day?

4. Even though you're traveling a hard road, are there still some small steps you could take in the direction of your dream? What are they?

Strategy #12: When You Come to the Jordan, Cross It

1. Have you passed up any opportunities to exit your wilderness? If so, what was that opportunity, and why did you pass it up? Is there any chance you could still claim it?

2. The Israelites still faced challenges, even after they left the wilderness. Can you look ahead and see problems on the horizon for you? What are they? How do you intend to deal with them?

3. God prepared the way for the Israelites to cross into the Promised Land and went ahead of them to protect them. Do you trust Him to do the same for you?

Strategy #13: Turn Your Trip into a Testimony

1. As you have traveled your hard road, have you received any help from someone who traveled it before you? What does that help mean to you?

2. Do you know someone who has recently landed on the same road you've been traveling? Are there some lessons you've learned that you feel would help that person? Is there anything that would keep you from sharing those lessons?

3. If you haven't already done so, are you willing to spend some time organizing and practicing your testimony so you can share it more effectively? Do you know someone who would be willing to help you?

About the Author

Mark Atteberry loves living in central Florida with his wife, Marilyn. In addition to preaching and writing, his great passions are sports and music. Mark loves to hear from his readers and invites you to contact him through his Web site, **markatteberry.net**. He is currently working on his fourth book for Thomas Nelson.

Acknowledgments

Albert Schweitzer said, "At times our own light goes out and is rekindled by a spark from another person. Each of us has cause to think with deep gratitude of those who have lighted the flame within us." The following is a partial list of the wonderful people who kept my flame burning during the writing of this book.

My wife, Marilyn, and my daughter, Michelle. I'm sure everybody wonders how an old bald-headed guy like me ended up with not one but two gorgeous women. What I love most is that they're even more beautiful on the inside.

My parents, Doug and Barbara Atteberry. Because they taught me to think, there will always be something of them in everything I write.

My agent, Lee Hough, of Alive Communications. He is a friend, adviser, cheerleader, comedian, philosopher, and personal representative all rolled into one. I only wish he was benefiting from our relationship as much as I am.

My acquisitions editor, Brian Hampton, at Nelson Books. Most authors will never get to work with someone of his stature even once, and now I've done it three times. I am truly blessed.

My editor, Kyle Olund, at Nelson Books. If I end up living in a nursing home, I hope they put me in the room next to a guy like Kyle. The man makes everything fun.

My friend and former professor, Keith McCaslin, of St. Louis Christian College. I doubt that anyone knows more about the Israelites' wilderness journey than Keith does. His keen insights got me over some difficult hurdles. (And to think . . . when I graduated in 1977, he thought he was rid of me.)

My friend JoDee McConnaughhay. A wonderful writer in her own right, JoDee and I went to college together and then didn't see each other for twenty-five years. My life is much richer because our paths crossed again.

My friend Mike Kocolowski. Mike read my book *The Samson Syndrome*, and found the courage to introduce himself to me, cold turkey, at a wedding reception. I had no idea that handshake would launch one of the greatest friendships of my life.

My friend Pat Williams of the Orlando Magic. The sports world knows Pat as the "Prince of the Ping Pong Balls." The Christian community knows him as a wonderful author. I know him as one of the nicest and most encouraging men I've ever met.

My flock, the members and friends of Poinciana Christian Church. They've listened to me preach almost every Sunday for sixteen years. Such patience should easily qualify them all for a beachfront condo in heaven.

And last, but certainly not least . . .

My friend, mentor, and hero, Karen Kingsbury. Karen is to writing what Babe Ruth is to baseball, only much better looking. More than anyone else, she is responsible for my writing career.

Notes

Strategy #5: Step over the Dead and Keep Going

1. Chip Ingram, *Love, Sex, and Lasting Relationships* (Grand Rapids: Baker, 2003), 160.

2. Words and music by Ira F. Stanphill, 1949.

Strategy #6: Trust God to Meet Your Needs

1. Elisabeth Elliot, *A Chance to Die: The Life and Legacy of Amy Carmichael* (Grand Rapids: Fleming H. Revell, 1987), 368–69.

2. Quoted by Kenneth Osbeck in *Amazing Grace* (Grand Rapids: Kregel, 1990), 27.

3. Eddie Rickenbacker, *Rickenbacker* (Englewood Cliffs, NJ: Prentice-Hall, 1967), 319.

4. Music by Walter Martin, lyrics by Civilla Martin. Written in 1904.

5. Evelyn Husband, *High Calling* (Nashville: Thomas Nelson, 2003), 232.

Strategy #7: Go at God's Pace

1. From the transcript of the film *The Donner Party*, by Ric Burns.

Strategy #8: Enjoy Every Oasis

1. John McCain, *Faith of My Fathers* (New York: Perennial, 2000), 314.

Strategy #9: Expect Detours

1. Rick Ezell, *Sightings of the Savior* (Downers Grove: InterVarsity, 2003), 22–23.

Strategy #11: Keep Your Dreams Alive

1. Derric Johnson, *The Wonder of America* (Tulsa: Honor Books, 1999), 170–71.

2. Bernadette Keaggy, *Losing You Too Soon* (Eugene, OR: Harvest House, 2002).

Strategy #13: Turn Your Trip into a Testimony

1. Information from Chicken Soup for the Soul Enterprises, found at www.chickensoup.com.

2. Craig Brian Larson, *Illustrations for Preaching and Teaching* (Grand Rapids: Baker, 2000), 5.

3. Cheryl McGuinness, *Beauty Beyond the Ashes* (West Monroe: Howard, 2004), 168–69.

Samson Struggled with More than Just a Bad Haircut . . .

The story of Samson is the perfect vehicle to reveal the twelve tendencies that can bring down strong men: disregarding their boundaries, struggling with lust, ignoring good advice, overestimating their own cleverness, and others. Written in a compassionate, funny, and practical style, *The Samson Syndrome* offers readers powerful ideas for making sure they use their greatest strengths to honor God in every situation. A study guide makes this perfect for individuals or groups to explore these themes on a deeper level.

ISBN 0-7852-6447-7

Want to See
Your Lifelong Dream Come True?

In *The Caleb Quest*, Mark Atteberry allows us to see that dreams don't come true by accident. On the contrary, fulfilled dreams are the result of clear thinking, strong faith, patience, and hard work. Geared to the everyday Christian, this biblical plan helps readers to test their dreams, identify "dream assassins," get God involved, accept His perfect timing, take action in pursuit of their dreams, and use their dreams to bless others.

ISBN 0-7852-6187-7